Really ^ Good Books for Kids

A Guide for Catechists and Parents

Janaan Manternach

Paulist Press
New York/Mahwah, N.J.

Cover and book design by Sharyn Banks

Library of Congress Cataloging-in-Publication Data

Manternach, Janaan.
   Really good books for kids: a guide for catechists and parents / Janaan Manternach.
      p. cm.
   Includes bibliographical references and index.
   ISBN 0–8091–4396–8 (alk. paper)
1. Christian literature for children—Bibliography. I. Title.
   Z7759.M36 2007
   [BR117.5]
   016.23—dc22

                                2006022036

Published by Paulist Press
997 Macarthur Boulevard
Mahwah, New Jersey 07430

www.paulistpress.com

Printed and bound in the
United States of America

CONTENTS

Dedicated to Carl J. Pfeifer,
my husband and best friend

INTRODUCTION

In her book *Reading Magic* (Harcourt, Inc., 2001), Mem Fox, the internationally respected literary expert and best-selling author, makes this startling claim: "If parents understood the huge educational benefits and intense happiness brought about by reading aloud to their children, and if every parent—and every adult caring for a child—read aloud a minimum of three stories a day to the children in their lives, we could probably wipe out illiteracy in one generation."

The book you have in front of you supports that very wise observation and does everything it can to equip parents, catechists, and teachers with titles of books in the context of religious and contemporary themes and seasons.

One of the greatest challenges that I've had in my long career as a professional catechist and teacher is to convince others—parents, teachers, and catechists—of the importance and value of story. Extensive experience has taught me that nothing instructs more than a story. Nothing inspires more than a story. Nothing stirs the imagination more than a story. Nothing provides greater moral guidance than a story. And nothing gives more joy to a child or young person than becoming friends with a story's character, entering into a story's adventure, and applauding and owning its outcome.

Often when I've prepared a lesson, whether for first graders, middle graders, teenagers, or adults, I've struggled with how to involve and engage them in such a way that they "get it," that they own the theological truths, the doctrines, the beliefs, the essential message. My question to myself is always, "What in this lesson will touch their spirits, will inspire, will move them to say Yes to the truth that is already in their hearts and minds and to the development of it that the lesson contains?"

And nearly always I have fallen back on children's literature for a story or poem that enhances, affirms, and tells, in an enticing, mystical, and literary way, a part of the lesson's story—a part that simply can't be presented and caught by any other exchange.

If you have a desire or even a slight temptation to start using more story in your religion classes or in your home, this book will be a great help. If it does nothing more than entice you to read more children's literature, that might be the best of all reasons for taking it in hand and using it.

1

STORIES
IN GENERAL

Stories Are Both Windows and Mirrors

In *Elijah at the Wedding Feast* (Acta Publications, 1999), John Shea succinctly describes story by telling how someone else described it: "As Murray Krieger pointed out, a story begins as a window. We are looking into the lives of others, into a world with which we are not familiar. In the course of the story, however, the window turns into a mirror. People who are not us show us to ourselves. We see ourselves in what is happening in others' lives."

In *The Art of Catechesis* (Paulist Press, 1998), Maureen Gallagher says practically the same thing. After quoting John Shea's reminder that "storytelling is the bedrock of human activity," she writes, "Good stories draw us out of our own little worlds. They help us live temporarily in another world with all its trials and tribulations, to be returned to our own actuality with new insights and more energy to cope with our lives."

I share John's and Maureen's belief that story, more than any other medium, educates, inspires, and transforms. It also resides

1

in our memories, becoming a resource that helps us become more human and holier.

Two stories that have the power to do all of that are *The Quiltmaker's Gift* by Jeff Brumbeau, illustrated by Gail de Marcken (Pfeifer-Hamilton, Inc., 2000) and *The Peddler's Gift* by Maxine Rose Schur, illustrated by Kimberly Roor Bulcken (Dial Books for Young Readers, 1999). *The Quiltmaker's Gift* is a charming fable that celebrates the joy of giving. But more than that, it's a story of how a very generous and creative quiltmaker helps a powerful and greedy king give his many things away and thus experience the goodness of sharing. Imaginative and richly colored illustrations by Gail de Marcken add immeasurably to the well-crafted text.

Two qualities that we hope will blossom and grow in our young are honor and kindness. *The Peddler's Gift* is a reminder that those two qualities are often found in unlikely places—in this instance, in a peddler who seems like a simpleton and is often the subject of mean gossip and disdainful amusement.

When the peddler arrives with his wares in the town of Korovenko, he goes to Leibush's home. Leibush's mother serves the peddler tea and honey cakes, after which he carefully lays out his wares. This visit is most unusual because, unlike at other times, the peddler's wares are varied and glorious. And among them are big four-sided Hanukkah tops called *dreidels*. One of the dreidels falls under a chair and the peddler seemingly doesn't notice. Leibush sees it and knows he should tell the peddler, but decides that it won't be missed and that he'll just borrow it. This quickly creates a moral dilemma for Leibush. How he and the peddler deal with it makes this story instructive and unforgettable.

Adults know from experience the strength of the human spirit, its flexibility, its capacity to cope, its power to persevere and to overcome. Children, too, have weathered personal losses and struggles, but for most of them, that experience lies in their futures. That's why stocking their memories now with stories about "overcoming" is critical in helping them to weather storms and "hang in" when the going gets tough. Here are two stories good for doing exactly that:

In the novel *Bud, Not Buddy* by Christopher Paul Curtis (Delacorte Press, 1999), Bud is a motherless boy on the run in search of his father. Once he decides to hit the road and find him, nothing can stop him. Whom Bud finds is not whom he expects to find, nor does that person expect what he discovers about Bud. Humaneness and grace flow through this story and are probably among the reasons it was awarded the Newbery Medal, given each year for the best in children's literature.

Another of this kind of story is *Hatchet* by Gary Paulsen (Bradbury, 1988). A plane in which a young boy is a passenger crashes. The pilot is killed and the boy is completely stranded. How he manages to survive is a powerful story of courage, ingenuity, tenacity, and perseverance. It, too, was awarded the Newbery Medal.

All of these books would be worthwhile additions to a parish's catechetical library or to the bookshelves of religious-education offices and/or local public libraries.

Story Connects Humanity to a Common Story and Ultimately to God

In 1985 I read *Storytelling: Imagination and Faith* by William J. Bausch (Twenty-Third Publications, 1984) and learned so much more about story and its value than I already knew. I recently read it again and relearned some of what I had discovered in my first reading and also much that I had missed. It's a valuable book for anyone engaged in faith work. The introduction begins with the observation: "Once upon a time, is no time and every time. It is the standard phrase that introduces us to other worlds and to our own world, that connects humanity to a common story and storyteller. That is why storytelling and story listening are so congenial, for, in one way or another, we are hearing about ourselves."

Here are some old favorite novels that do what's described above. They are stories that provide an intractable "knowledge energy" linking one person to another, one generation to another, and ultimately all to God.

The Cay by Theodore Taylor (Avon Books, 1970). Philip has looked down upon black-skinned people all his life. Suddenly, he's a refugee from a fatal shipwreck and dependent on an extraordinary West Indian named Timothy. The two of them are cast up on a barren Caribbean island. A crack on his head has left Philip blind.

The story connects us with their struggle for survival, and with the boy's efforts to adjust to blindness and to understand the dignified, wise, and loving man who is his companion. I read this story a long time ago and it lingers in my memory, a source of inspiration and a challenge to my own prejudices.

In *The Witch of Blackbird Pond* by Elizabeth George Speare (Bantam Doubleday Dell, 1987)—a Newbery Medal winner— Kit Tyler is facing life on the cold, bleak shores of Connecticut Colony. Her new home is a far cry from the luxury and the climate she enjoyed in the shimmering Caribbean islands. She's like a tropical bird that has flown to the wrong part of the world. In the stern Puritan community of her relatives, she feels caged and lonely. The only place where she feels completely free is in the meadows. There she meets another lone and mysterious figure, the old woman known as the Witch of Blackbird Pond. But when their friendship is discovered, Kit is faced with suspicion, fear, anger, and a witch trial.

The story renews one's sense of the pleasure that reading children's literature provides. I enjoyed it so much that, for a while, I hesitated to read another piece because I was afraid of a letdown.

Island of the Blue Dolphins by Scott O'Dell (Bantam Doubleday Dell, 1987)—another Newbery Medal winner—tells the story of Karana, a Native American girl, who lives alone for years on the Island of the Blue Dolphins. Year after year she watches one season pass into another and waits for a ship to take her away. While she waits, she keeps herself alive by building shelters, making weapons, finding food, and fighting off the wild dogs.

This is one of the most powerful pieces of children's literature I have ever read. Karana's unselfishness and courage inspire and stir the imagination to wonder continually, "What if she had made another choice?"

In *Lyddie* by Katherine Paterson (Penguin Books, 1991), Lyddie Worthen is completely on her own. Her parents are gone and her brother and sisters are living with other people. When Lyddie hears about the mill jobs in Lowell, Massachusetts, she heads there with the goal of earning enough money to reunite her family. Six days a week from dawn to dusk, Lyddie and the other girls run weaving looms in the dusty and lint-filled factory. Lyddie learns to read and to handle the menacing overseer. But when the working conditions begin to affect her friends' health, she has to make a choice. Will she speak up for better working conditions and risk her job and her dream? Or will she stay quiet until it is perhaps too late? Though not a medal winner, this is a superb story of grit, determination, and personal growth.

Reading good literature makes us more thoughtful, perceptive, compassionate, caring—ultimately more human. Stories are a gift that we can and need to give to ourselves and our children.

Story and Catechesis

I am passionate about story—especially about story in catechesis. Story instructs, awakens, inspires, stirs imaginations, motivates, and lodges itself in our memories, thus becoming a hidden and latent power.

Clifton Fadiman puts his finger on the special power of story: "When you read a classic, you do not see in the book more than you did before. You see more in you than there was before." As we see more into our own lives through story, we become more open to God's story unfolding in our lives.

One way to encourage catechists is to model the use of story during in-service sessions. My husband, Carl Pfeifer, and I use stories in every in-service session, workshop, and talk that we give—as well as in the actual catechesis of young and old alike. We find that adults who experience a story's power within a catechetical moment feel more open to using stories in their own catechetical sessions.

Stories abound in bookstores and libraries, but not all stories have catechetical potential. So catechists need some knowledge of children's literature and some skill in making a story work within a lesson. A story needs to enhance a lesson's faith theme by unveiling life's deeper mysteries. It needs to have, as its essence, elements of what is to be learned. And it has to be written and/or visualized in a fascinating, delightful, and beautiful way.

A good way to become a discerner of good stories is to read lots of children's and young adults' literature. A good place to start reading is with the annual Newbery Medal and Honor books. Each year the best novels for children and youth are singled out for these prestigious awards. These books are always "in print." Libraries often have special listings of them, and bookstores frequently display them on a special rack. They are fine books for acquiring a taste for reading children's literature. Here are some examples.

Crispin by Avi (Hyperion Books for Children, 2002) is a John Newbery Award winner, an unforgettable novel about a young teenager who loses everything—home, family, possessions. He is also accused of a crime he didn't commit. Furthermore, he is declared a "wolf's head," which means he may be killed on sight. One of the more amazing things about the story is how the boy constantly turns to prayer using a lead cross that was his mother's.

The Newbery Medal book *Out of the Dust* by Karen Hesse (Scholastic Press, 1997) is about real sorrow, real struggle, resurrection borne out of hope, and a deep ownership of self. As with *Crispin*, this story, too, is unforgettable. It causes us to wonder continually how the main character, Billie Jo, managed to deal with and survive all that she endured despite her young age. This, in itself, adds depth to our awareness of how unbelievably strong is the human spirit.

All of us, not just our children, need this kind of nurture to keep us going through the challenges and hardships that are part of our own stories. In theological terms *Out of the Dust* is about death and resurrection.

Two more Newbery Medal winners are worth recommending to your catechists.

In *The Matchlock Gun* by Walter D. Edmonds (Penguin Putnam Books for Young Readers, 1998; Newbery, 1942) a ten-year-old boy, left to protect his mother and little sister, courageously and with perfect timing, fires a huge matchlock gun and saves them.

Shiloh by Phyllis Reynolds Naylor (Bantam Doubleday Dell, 1992; Newbery, 1992) tells the story of a boy's willingness to do anything to save an abused dog from its cruel owner. In theological terms this is a salvation story.

While not a Newbery winner as he wrote and illustrated picture books, an author tailor-made for catechetical lessons is Leo Lionni, a giant in the field of children's literature. He didn't begin his children's books career until he was almost fifty, then he went on to write and illustrate more than forty books.

I discovered Leo Lionni in the early 1960s while searching for stories to use with a first communion class, and happened upon his first children's book, *Little Blue and Little Yellow* (Astor Honor Publishing, 1959; Mulberry Books, 1995). Two spots, named Little Blue and Little Yellow, are sharing a wonderful adventure. Their friendship is so close that it changes them into one color, green. When their parents see them, they don't understand what has happened until they also experience the changing union that their sons enjoyed. It's an imaginative story that, for me, symbolizes the change that occurs through friendship with another and also through union with Jesus. When using it with seven-year-olds, I find that Lionni's visual presentation, along with his brief and lively text, opens up for them the profound mystery of Eucharist. Actually, after reading the story with one group, a child spontaneously remarked, "I think that's kind of what will happen to us when we make our first communion."

Anthologies and Catechesis

Catechists and religion teachers, willing and eager to use story in their classes, have told me that they don't feel comfortable taking ten to fifteen minutes of class time for story, and that the shorter stories I recommend are not available in their local libraries or bookstores. I understand their feelings and frustration, and have searched for more readily available books that have tales in them that fit religious themes. Anthologies are perfect for this use.

Hey! Listen to This by Jim Trelease (Penguin Books, 1996) contains forty-eight read-aloud stories that parents and teachers can share with children aged five through nine.

In their own description of the best-seller *Chicken Soup for the Soul*, compilers Jack Canfield and Mark Victor Hansen (Health Communications, 1993) say, "Whenever you wish to make a point, inspire a friend, or teach a child, you'll find just the right story in this heartwarming treasury." And perhaps better suited for the age range is their collection *Chicken Soup for the Kid's Soul*, Jack Canfield and Mark Victor Hansen, this time with Patty Hansen and Irene Dunlap (Health Communications, Inc., 1998). The stories are categorized according to themes of love, friendship, family, attitude and perspective, death and dying, achieving dreams, overcoming obstacles, choices, tough stuff, and eclectic wisdom. Many of the stories are written by children themselves, and others are written by adults about experiences during their childhood. Surprisingly, many of them identify God's presence and help and express the belief that God can be trusted and depended upon. Community and sacrifice, central themes in our Catholic Christian tradition, are also reflected in many stories; for example, "The Tower," "The Visit," and "The Fire Truck," in the first section alone. I recommend buying several copies for the religious education library or providing a copy for each class.

For older kids, there's *Chicken Soup for the Teenage Soul* by Jack Canfield, Mark Victor Hansen, and Kimberly Kirberger (Health Communications, Inc., 1997).

A set of books on my library shelf that I've referred to often while planning religion classes are the "Virtue" books compiled by William Bennett. *The Children's Book of Virtues*, illustrated by Michael Hague (Simon & Schuster, 1995), is for younger children. Three of my favorites here are "The King and His Hawk," retold by James Baldwin; "St. George and the Dragon," retold by J. Berg Esenwein and Marietta Stockard; and "Someone Sees You." Another of the stories, "The Sermon to the Birds," also retold by James Baldwin, is about St. Francis of Assisi and is a good one to read on or near October 4th, his feast day.

The Book of Virtues for Young People by William Bennett (Silver Burdett Press, 1996), another of the series, is full of wonderful tales, many of which have surprise endings, such as "The Chest of Broken Glass" and "The Sword of Damocles," adapted from James Baldwin.

The most comprehensive book in the series is the first, *The Book of Virtues: A Treasury of Great Moral Stories* (Simon & Schuster, 1993). It contains fairy tales, myths, and many stories about biblical characters. All three books contain poetry, fables, and prayers. I mention other anthologies by Bennett under their appropriate chapter.

Finally, a collection of short stories that is truly my all-time favorite for adults and children is Leo Lionni's *Frederick's Fables* (Pantheon Books, 1985). This brings together thirteen of his best-loved picture books, including some that received the Caldecott Honor for their illustrations. An added gift in this book is its introduction by Bruno Bettelheim, in which he describes the value of picture books for young children. The introduction is a great tribute because Bettelheim understood well Lionni's genius of conveying reality through imaginative images and little text. My three favorites from the collection are *Swimmy, Tico and the Golden Wings*, and *Frederick*.

Swimmy is another story (like *Little Blue and Little Yellow*, mentioned above) often used with children preparing for first

Eucharist. Swimmy, a little fish, creatively devises a plan in which a school of fish swim together as one big fish and chase away the big fish they fear. It's a stunning story about the power of acting together as a community.

In every group, there are children singled out because they are different, which causes them much pain. Lionni deals with this issue in *Tico and the Golden Wings*. Tico is born without wings, but in this story, his friends, with wings, love him and take care of him. However, he longs for wings and one day his wish is granted. But because of his wish, his wings are golden, not black like those of his friends. This makes them unhappy with Tico and they fly away, leaving him alone. What he does with his golden wings and how he changes because of his behavior are the best and most moving parts of the story. Children easily identify with Tico's hopes and wishes. And even though the inference is subtle, most children understand why Tico is still different, even though his wings are now black like the other birds.

Another favorite is *Frederick*. Frederick, a field mouse, is contemplative by nature. While the other field mice gather corn and nuts and wheat and straw, Frederick sits quietly, gathering into his mind and heart the rays of the sun, the colors of the meadow, and words, for he is also a poet. The tale ends when the mice are fed, after the other food runs out, by the things that Frederick gathered.

All of these anthologies would be valuable additions to your religious education library and good ones to recommend to parents as gifts for their children. They could also be a starter set for a child's personal bookshelf.

2

RESURRECTION STORIES

The Threads of Life Are Woven in Story

In *How Creative Catechists Use Stories* (Twenty-Third Publications, 2000), Carl Pfeifer and I address the importance of story as an instructional tool. We also give suggestions for using story in creative and meaningful ways. We stress that story deals with every aspect of the human and divine, that it lodges itself in the memory, that it heals, and most importantly, that Jesus used it.

Story is a powerful resource for learning how kids are kids and what life is like for them. What is true of all of us—that we talk to ourselves all the time—is equally true of children and young people. Story gives us ears to hear it. The self-talk in story reveals hidden fears, hidden ways of coping or failing to cope, and hidden paths of survival or destruction. Also revealed are the roles that friends, enemies, parents, teachers, and other adults play, as well as the confusion, frustrations, failures, successes, joys, and discoveries that happen along the way.

I believe strongly that all of us who live or work with children and young people need to read literature written for and about them and need to do it early in a new catechetical or academic year. This literature, more than anything else, puts us in touch with the stories that young people are writing in their dreams, spirits, and everyday lives.

After reading a story about bullying in *The Washington Post* (May 8, 2001), ninth-grader Nickolaus Johnston of Manassas, Virginia, wrote a letter to the editor in which he said that he had been a victim of bullying his whole life. He wrote:

> People make fun of others to be popular, and when the popular person does it, others have to do it, too....This results in torture for the victim and causes extreme anger to be held inside....Some people are able to hold the anger in, but the Columbine incident showed how some people who can't go insane. They want to kill the people to pay them back.

He then complains,

> Some experts say to ignore bullies. That has to be the stupidest advice on the planet. It does nothing. Also, if adults think that kids need to be more assertive or tough, they won't accept that their child is doing something wrong by bullying. Saying that being bullied is part of growing up is like saying that being emotionally harassed is part of growing up....[He ends his letter:] My suggestion is to have a professional observe students' class behavior and at recess to recognize who is being ridiculed.

In light of that I strongly recommend two books: *On the Fringe*, edited by Donald R. Gallo (Dial Books, 2001), and *Hope Was Here* by Joan Bauer (G. P. Putnam's Sons, 2000).

On the Fringe is a collection of stories about teens who are "outsiders." The stories offer insights into popularity and peer pressure, nonconformity and persecution, acceptance and hate. The dedication for the book says, "This book is dedicated to every kid who has ever been called a hateful name. And to every kid who has tried to feel superior by putting down someone else."

It is a painful read, but its insights made it possible for me to keep reading even when I felt I couldn't continue. A significant part of the book is the identification of other stories by each author, especially those that have won awards and/or are listed in the *100 Best Books for Young Adults* and the *100 Best Children's Books*.

Hope Was Here is an easier read. It's about Addie, a sixteen-year-old who lives with her aunt. They travel a lot, which means that Hope (she changes her name along the way) never gets to stay in one place very long, and that's tough. Their latest move threatens to be the hardest yet, but during it Hope meets politics, corruption, and her past head-on. It's a delightful story about honor, trust, and serving up your very best.

Remember that Nickolaus Johnston said that he was bullied all his life. That's true for many children. Therefore, it's good to become aware and alert even with the youngest children.

Story is a good place to start.

The Threads of Faith Are Woven in Story

Henri J. Nouwen is a familiar and much-loved author of books that have the power to enrich and deepen faith. In reading a new printing of Nouwen's *Here and Now: Living in the Spirit*

(Crossroad, 2000), I'm reminded again of how close God is—much closer than we usually realize, Nouwen suggests.

In the book he also writes about choosing joy in the midst of sorrow, about disciplined living, prayer, compassion, friendship, family, and the lifelong process of conversion. As I read, I was inspired in such a way that changes have occurred in my faith life. One of his recommendations is to continually read books that enhance and deepen who we are and how we believe.

It's important for children and young people as well to read books and to hear stories that deepen their faith and stir their spirits. Here are some that I recommend:

The Children's Book of Faith by William J. Bennett (Random House Children's Books, 2000) contains stories from the Bible, tales of great and admirable people, prayers, poetry, and song. The author describes the aim of the book as an aid "to help youngsters learn that we all belong to the Almighty and that we must strive in ways that glorify him."

In God's Name by Sandy Eisenberg Sasso (Jewish Lights Publishing, 1994) is an exquisite book in which many different people give God a name until finally they all settle on a "perfect" one.

God Said Amen by Sandy Eisenberg Sasso (Jewish Lights Publishing, 2000) tells of two rulers, a prince and a princess, who each have a big problem. The kingdom of the princess is overflowing with oil but needs water. The kingdom of the prince has water but needs oil. They both ask God for help, but they prove too stubborn and full of pride to reach out to ask each other for what they need. Both kingdoms are eventually saved, but not by the prince or princess.

In *Jesus* by Brian Wildsmith (Eerdmans Books for Young Readers, 2000), an unusually beautiful picture book, the author portrays the life of Jesus of Nazareth in a series of wonderful scenes, framed by gold. The "seeing" that can happen while reading this book may place an indelible memory in a child's mind, heart, and spirit.

The little book *Day of the Dead* by Tony Johnston (Harcourt Brace & Co., 1997) gives children a visual and verbal experience of one of Mexico's most important holidays, *El Día de los Muertos*. The holiday spans three days, from October 31 to November 2, and is a time to remember loved ones now gone. With the book as a backdrop, a conversation might take place in which the children tell how they remember loved ones now gone.

Rock Steady by Sting (HarperCollins Publishers, 1987) is a modern spin on the tale of Noah's Ark. Adapting the lyrics of his own song, Sting creates a version of the story that is a reminder that human beings are blessed, and that we must protect the earth that has given us life.

A *Tale from Paleface Creek* by Robert Morneau (Paulist Press, 2000) has the qualities of a fable and the instructional flavor of wisdom literature. Barry the Beaver works, works, works. Working is the sum and substance of his whole existence until he finds himself reaching out to friends and to possibilities beyond working all the time. How he responds to what he hears changes not only his own life but his wife's and children's as well.

Sometimes the most important task for young people is to develop faith in themselves—in who they are and what they'd like to become. Some of the best literature for young people tells that kind of story. One worth reading is *Backwater* by Joan Bauer (Puffin Books, 1999).

Main character Ivy is part of a family in which becoming a lawyer is the expected goal. Her father is one of the best, and he can't imagine any other possibility for his daughter. Yet Ivy, a "historian" at heart, and also by some practice, is not at all cut out to be a lawyer. How she gradually owns who she really is and wins over her father is an unforgettable tale of growing up and staying true to oneself.

The Threads of Caring Are Woven in Story

My dear friend Frank Gross of Kalamazoo, Michigan, wrote *The Gospels with Salt* (Hamilton Books, 2005), and in that book he refers to a question and answer that inspired him: "What did the lama say about doing something about the long history of hatred? 'Take a friend to lunch.'"

As I think about that powerful suggestion my thoughts keep zoning in on *caring*.

If we examine our habits of caring, we might decide to keep doing the caring we do well, change one or other habit in which we are careless, and add one or more caring habits to our repertoire. And still another thing we might do is fill our children's minds and hearts with stories in which caring makes all the difference in the lives of others.

A superb piece, one of the best that I have read in a long time, is *Jake's Orphan* by Peggy Brooke (Dorling Kindersley Publishing, Inc., 2000). The year of this story is 1926 and the setting is on the untamed North Dakota prairie. Two brothers are in an orphanage. Tree, the older one, longs to escape the place and find a home for himself and his brother. But when his chance finally comes, the adoptive family wants only one boy to help work their farm. Tree promises his younger brother, Acorn, "If I don't come back, I'll send for you."

Yet nothing Tree does wins over the farmer who is harsh, cruel, and unrelenting in his criticism. Tree's solemn promise seems impossible to keep—except that the farmer's brother, Jake, also lives on the farm. His kind ways give Tree hope, and all is going well until Acorn suddenly appears and threatens everything. In the end, however, Tree, with Jake's help, is finally able to keep his promise. It's a powerful story of cruelty and unexpected kindness, of loyalty and thoughtless betrayal, of blustering cowardice and quiet courage, and of the kind of caring that is embracing, touching, and redeeming.

Another story, different but as powerful, is *Letters from Rifka* by Karen Hesse (Puffin Books, 1993). Written by the winner of the 1998 Newbery Award–winning *Out of the Dust*, this story is about a Jewish family fleeing Russia's brutal treatment for a new life in America. The path to freedom is full of terrible obstacles. The family is seemingly at last victorious until it's time to board the ship for America. The doctors refuse to let twelve-year-old Rifka board and the family has to leave without her. One way Rifka deals with having to stay behind is to write letters to her cousin Tovah, in which she records everything that happens to her.

Near the end of her journey Rifka meets Ilya, a seven-year-old peasant boy who is Russian. He symbolizes everything that has made her life and her family's so miserable. How she overcomes her feelings and helps Ilya is the kind of caring that is nothing less than sacred. Because of her compassion, both Rifka and Ilya are permitted to enter the country and to stay in America. Overcoming justified hate, as did Rifka, is the most powerful of kind of caring.

Sometimes the caring we need to do is repenting for our past—a past in which other human beings were enslaved and treated cruelly. A story that might help us and our children see reasons for repenting is *The Secret to Freedom* by Marcia Vaughn (Lee & Low Books, Inc., 2001). This is a story that a grandmother tells her granddaughter in response to a question about a piece of quilt that is hanging in the kitchen.

When the grandmother was a girl, her parents are sold off the plantation and she never sees them again. Along with her brother, she continues to work on the plantation for a cruel master.

Her brother comes home one evening with something that can make a difference—a sack of quilts. The quilts are used to give vital information to slaves planning to escape on the Underground Railroad. With the urging of his sister, the brother escapes. She is unsure that she will ever see him again until one day a letter arrives with the piece of quilt that the granddaughter sees in the kitchen. The book is a story of a brother who cares about freedom for others and a sister who cares for the safety of her brother. It's a story that gives a glimpse of a painful part of our American history.

There are many pieces of children's literature in which caring is the central theme. Discover other titles in your local library or children's bookstore.

The Threads of Holiness Are Woven in Story

Recently when my husband and I were in Iowa, we visited with our niece Diane Boardman, and her son, Kyle. I asked Kyle what his favorite book is. He totally surprised us by answering, *New Picture Book of Saints*. It's by Rev. Lawrence G. Lovasik, SVD (Catholic Book Publishing Company, 1979). My next question was, "Who is your favorite?" He quickly named Francis of Assisi. When we asked him about others like Dominic Savio, Elizabeth Ann Seton, Joan of Arc, and Martin of Tours, he told us things about them also.

Because I was still feeling skeptical about his enthusiasm, I asked him what he knew about Francis of Assisi. He had practically memorized what he had read in the book. And he had also done a project about Francis in school.

To say the least, I still find it unusual that a nine-year-old is so turned on to stories of the saints. But Kyle, a delightfully ordinary boy who has read *Holes* by Louis Sachar (Farrar, Straus and Giroux, 1998) at least twice, has an extraordinary love for the saints. His mother said that he reads their stories over and over.

The experience awakened me to the truth that holiness is attractive to children and young people. It also inspired me to read some of the saints books in my personal collection. Here are three of my favorites:

The Treasury of Saints and Martyrs by Margaret Mulvihill (Penguin Books for Young Readers, 1999) is a wonderfully illustrated book that includes stories of more than fifty saints and martyrs. It's unique in that it offers personal histories of each saint, tales of their most famous deeds, and information on patron saints. A feature that I really like is the many miniature black-and-white drawings that add information in a creative sidebar style.

Both *Saint Francis* (1995) and *Joseph* (1997) by Brian Wildsmith (Wm. B. Eerdmans Publishing Co.) are beautifully illustrated and sensitively written. They would be worthwhile additions to school and religious education libraries and wonderful gifts for a child's home library.

Kyle's obvious fascination with sanctity pushed me to look for shades of holiness in stories other than those about canonized saints. I was delighted with the discovery that, like the saints, the heroes and heroines in these stories are caring and unselfish, deal with major challenges, make great sacrifices, and refuse to be overcome by evil. Here are a few such books that I strongly recommend:

The Children's Book of America by William J. Bennett (Simon & Schuster, 1998) is a treasury of folktales, songs, and poems, celebrating both heroes and everyday Americans. Some of the former are Father Junipero Serra, Abigail Adams, Paul Bunyan, Johnny Appleseed, Robert E. Lee, Abraham Lincoln, Martin Luther King, Jr., and Margaret of Orleans.

Let It Shine: Stories of Black Women Freedom Fighters by Andrea Davis Pinckney (Gulliver Books, 2000) is about courage in the face of inequality, oppression, prejudice, and fear. It's about the challenges and triumphs of the battle for civil rights, and it's about speaking out for what you believe, even when it feels as if no one is listening. The women who are featured in this book include Sojourner Truth, Biddy Mason, Harriet Tubman, Ida B. Wells Barnett, Rosa Parks, Fannie Lou Hamer, and Shirley Chisholm.

The Butterfly by Patricia Polacco (Philomel Books, 2000) is based on the lives of the author's Aunt Monique and Monique's mother, Marcel Solliliage, who, during the French Resistance, helped Jews escape to freedom from the Nazi regime. Gently narrated, this story reveals the horror of that time and the courage of people willing to risk their lives to save others.

In the Moonlight Mist by Daniel San Souci (Boyds Mill Press, 1999) is a retelling of one of Korea's most beloved stories about a woodcutter, his wife, his child, his mother, and a deer. The woodcutter wasn't good at following instructions but he cared about animals and protected them. He also loved his mother enough to sacrifice, for her, what he wanted more than anything else.

All of us, including children and young people, can learn a lot about holiness from the above-named and other spirited stories. Reading has the power to deepen and transform.

The Threads of Endurance Are Woven in Story

A year I will never forget is one that was filled with hard times. It started with the sudden death of my sister's beloved friend in a plane crash, then the suicide of the son of a long-time friend, followed by the return of cancer in another friend, and finally a series of doctor visits to determine the cause of a health problem in a family member.

Easter helps us to consider hard times and to rejoice in the resurrections that often flow from them, again and again. A powerful example is *The Straight Story*, a true story made into a movie. Alvin Straight, played by Richard Farnsworth, is a no-nonsense, independent man. He's at an age when he can't drive because of poor eyesight, needs two canes to help him walk, and lives a quiet life with his daughter Rose (Sissy Spacek). But when the call comes that his estranged brother, Lyle (Harry Dean Stanton), has suffered a stroke, Alvin puts aside his frailties and embarks on a dangerous and emotional journey to make amends. With little money but plenty of patience and tenacity, he climbs aboard his John Deere lawnmower and travels the 260 miles from his small Iowa town to Lyle's home in Wisconsin.

Filmed along the actual route that the real Alvin Straight traveled in 1994, *The Straight Story* chronicles his six-week odyssey, during which he touches many lives and shares the regret that he and his brother have not been brothers for ten years. The journey is painfully slow. It takes everything Alvin has to keep going, but he makes it. The reunion of the brothers is quiet and healing. Richard Farnsworth was nominated in the Best Actor category for the Academy Awards and the movie won the 1999 Screen International Award.

This same odyssey, this same triumph of spirit, is found in children's literature. For example, in *A Year Down Yonder* by

Richard Peck (Dial Books, 2000), fifteen-year-old Mary Alice faces a whole year with her grandmother, a woman who seemingly doesn't "have a hug in her." The situation is hard for Mary Alice, but gradually she grows to respect and love her grandmother and eventually describes her as having "eyes in the back of her heart." Nothing during the whole year is easy, but the ending is surprising, happy, and satisfying. This book won the prestigious John Newbery Medal in 2001.

Kate DiCamillo's *Because of Winn-Dixie* (Candlewick Press, 2000) tells the story of ten-year-old India Opal Buloni, who has just moved to Naomi, Florida, with her preacher father. She doesn't know what to expect—least of all that she'll adopt a dog she names Winn-Dixie after the supermarket where they meet. Opal finds that she can tell Winn-Dixie everything, such as how much she's been thinking about her mother, who left when she was three, and that she's lonely.

Opal needs friends and, because of Winn-Dixie, she finds herself making a few. Gradually she gets her father to tell her about her mother, and during a party in which Winn-Dixie seems to be lost, Opal and her father come to a greater understanding of the losses and the blessings in their lives. It's a poignant story involving a child's relationship with her father, a friendly dog, and some unusual friends (Newbery Honor Book, 2001).

In the Chinese folktale *The Hunter* by Mary Casanova (Atheneum Books, 2000), Hai Li Bu, a young hunter, is unable to find enough food for his village when a drought comes. One day, while hunting, he saves the life of a small snake. The snake's father, the Dragon King, offers to give him anything. All Hai Li Bu wants is to provide better for his village. He tells the Dragon King, "The only thing I desire is to understand the language of animals. Then I can be a better hunter." The Dragon King gives Hai Li Bu a round stone, tells him to take it and his wish will come true, but warns him that he must not pass on the secret of the gift or he will surely turn to stone.

When the animals tell Hai Li Bu that a storm will flood his village, he tries to warn the villagers but they do not believe him. Realizing the danger, he knows that he can flee and save himself or give up his secret and lose his life. What he chooses is still remembered in China.

3

CHRISTMAS STORIES

Stories of Gifts for Advent and Christmas

Nine months had passed since Christmas when I met my dear friend, Susan Keys, for tea and muffins at a local French café. With her were gifts that she had intended to give me the previous Christmas. Every time in between, when we had seen each other, she had forgotten to bring the gifts.

The gifts are lovely—a handmade angel ornament, and a candle and holder. But what surprises me more than the gifts themselves is the delight I feel about them. They symbolize a friendship that has grown over the years and that nurtures both of us, even when we don't see each other for a while. When too much time elapses in between our getting together, we find ourselves e-mailing and phoning to set up a time to meet.

As I pondered the gifts and our friendship, I found myself with a more generous point of view regarding Advent and what many of us do during the season. We're preoccupied with "gifts." I know that this preoccupation is often a hassle, but put into the context of the "gift" of Jesus' coming, it's a near perfect way to live out Advent in preparation for Christmas.

With this in mind, I went through my collection of Christmas stories and was amazed at how many of them have the word *gift* in their titles. Using stories like these in our catechetical settings can help us connect the wondrous and sacred mystery of Christmas with the wonder and joy of "gifts." A few of them that I've read again and again and use at Christmastime with children and adults are named and described below.

The Best Gift of All by Cornelia Wilkeshuis (St. Paul Books & Media, 1989) tells of Prince Irenus, the young son of King Balthasar, who decides to follow the star with his father so that he can also see the new Prince. He knows his father is taking a golden goblet as a gift, so Irenus decides to take along his red bouncing ball, his favorite book, and his beloved dog, Pluton. He's not sure he'll be able to give up his pet but he sets out with that in mind. On the way, he finds others who need his gifts and when he arrives at the stable, he has nothing left to give to the Prince of Peace.

This is a wonderful story to act out. One Christmas, as part of the homily, children at Our Lady Queen of Peace Church in Arlington, Virginia, dramatized the story to the congregation's inspiration and delight.

In *The Best Gift for Mom* by Lee Klein, illustrated by Pamela T. Keating (Paulist Press, 1995), Jonathan's father is dead. One evening after Jonathan has lied about his father's death, his mother tells him about how his father died so he won't have to lie about it anymore. Then Jonathan remembers how his father used to put him to sleep when he was little. Using that memory, he gives his mother a special Christmas gift.

The Gift of the Magi by O. Henry, illustrated by Lisbeth Zwerger (Picture Book Studio, 1982) is a classic story of a young couple who are very poor. It's Christmas Eve and each wants to give the other a longed-for present. How they manage to buy the gifts is a story of amazing sacrifice and deep love; it's also a story with an ending that is both exquisite and touching.

Littlejim's Gift by Gloria Houston (Philomel Books, 1994) is one of my favorite Christmas stories. Times are hard, the country is at war, and Littlejim's father considers Christmas as just another day. But deep down Littlejim can't help wishing that his family can go to the church Christmas tree celebration. He wants his family to share the feeling of Christmas. He saves his pennies, helps his mother with chores, runs errands with his sister Nell, all the time wishing, wishing, wishing. Finally, he realizes that the best part of Christmas is the giving part. But with his father beside him and the gift he most wants in his hand, he also feels the wonder and joy of receiving.

Many Christmas stories don't have the word *gift* in their titles but are also about giving. Spend time reading and choosing some of them to enjoy and to share.

Christmas Is a Time for Tales about the Needy

An article in *The Washington Post* titled "New York's Homeless Get Prison for Shelter" (August 16, 2002) described the awful circumstances under which many homeless families were being housed. The reason given was that, fed by a weak economy and a dearth of affordable housing, the number of men, women, and children crammed into New York's shelters and welfare hotels had reached record numbers; the homeless census then stood at 34,500.

The article also reported that the problem was not confined to New York. In Massachusetts, Connecticut, and the District of Columbia, record numbers of homeless families had sought shelter during the previous summer, in numbers typically seen only in the harshest winter months.

Needing something as basic as housing is a reality that might well be connected with the story of Joseph and Mary who faced "no room in the inn." Unfortunately a lack of housing is not the only need that is felt by many at Christmastime. Emotional and spiritual needs often lie beneath the surface or alongside the merriment, gifts, parties, and decorations. Therefore, it's not surprising that so many Christmas stories are about "not having."

Here are some of the best of these stories:

The Christmas Promise by Susan Bartoletti (Blue Sky Press, 2001) touches on the misery of the Great Depression in the United States in 1929 and 1930. Over a million men, women, and children became wanderers known as hoboes. In this story, an impoverished father and his daughter are forced by circumstances to sneak into open box cars and ride from town to town looking for work. When no work is found, they band together with other hoboes for food. Gradually the young girl learns how to read hobo signs chalked beneath railroad bridges.

When winter comes, it's too cold for the child. Her father finds her a place to stay but promises to return as soon as he finds work. And before the first Christmas star comes out, he does. This is a story that teaches more than the plight of a father and daughter during the Depression. It's about the love they share and the trust between them that proves to be the most valuable of Christmas gifts.

In *The Shine Man* by Mary Quattlebaum (Eerdman Books for Young Readers, 2001), it's the Christmas of 1932. Money is tight, so tight that no one can afford even a nickel for a shoeshine. Larry, the shoeshine man, tries to drum up business in the bitter cold, but no one stops. When nothing happens, he notices a bit of trash and makes a spoolie, a Christmas angel, out of spools, some cloth scraps, and a tuft of yarn.

Seeing the spoolie, a child wants it, but the Shine Man realizes the boy needs a cap more and gives him his. Gradually he also gives him his gloves; eventually even the spoolie. Last, he gives the child the best shoe shine ever. What happens next is a glimpse of the transforming power of giving.

The Shoe Tree of Chagrin by J. Patrick Lewis (Creative Editions, 2001) is a story about Susannah DeClare, the tallest of the great plains women who traveled the Ohio Valley. She made shoes with such care that they lasted their owners a lifetime. Her days were spent traveling from town to town taking orders, making shoes, and delivering them. She never failed to show up when she promised, until one Christmas. A strange postcard arrived at the Gifford cottage with a message that took the children of Chagrin to a tree near the end of the gravel road. On it hung the shoes that had been ordered, her boots, and the horseshoes of PawPaw, who had faithfully pulled her wagon. It's a splendid tale of friendship, trust, and the unexpected.

The Christmas Cross by Max Lucado (Word Publishing, Inc., 1998) is a story for adults—a gift you might give yourself. It's about mistakes and mercy and Christmas miracles.

Story has a unique power to soothe Christmas hungers in children. The best catechesis for the season is to read aloud with lavish expression any of the splendid and available Christmas tales. They need not be the ones described here—choose ones you like and give your children a great gift.

Books Make Great Christmas Gifts

On two Sundays during a recent December my husband, Carl Pfeifer, and I gave talks on preparing for Christmas as part of our parish's adult education series. As usual, we mentioned titles from children's literature and gave out bibliographies. What surprised us was the keen interest in suggestions for books adults might give as Christmas gifts not just to children but also to friends. They were especially interested in books to read for themselves. In the fast-paced world in which most adults live, they yearned for something that would help them observe Advent and prepare for Christmas peacefully, productively, and with less stress.

One of the best of these is *Unplug the Christmas Machine: A Complete Guide to Putting Love and Joy Back into the Season* by Jo Robinson and Jean Coppock Staeheli (William Morrow, 1991, revised edition). It offers meaningful and practical suggestions for combating commercialism and filling the holidays with simple spiritual celebrations that help families draw closer together. It's a perfect gift for adults to buy and read before they begin their Christmas entertaining and shopping.

Another book that adults might give themselves is *The Christmas Box* by Richard Paul Evans (Simon and Schuster, 1993). It's a quick read that pinpoints love as the energy and challenge within the meaning of Christmas.

How Creative Catechists Use Stories by Janaan Manternach and Carl J. Pfeifer (Twenty-Third Publications, 2001) is another great book. Two of the chapters in the book are on Advent and Christmas. Each contains reflections and stories that gently and simply immerse the reader in the seasons. Additionally, Advent and Christmas stories in children's literature are named and briefly described. This might be a perfect Christmas gift for catechists and religion teachers who give so much to children and young people in school and parish programs.

For children a delightful Christmas book is *Gloria the Christmas Angel* by Scott Anthony Asalone (Treehaus Communications, Inc., 2000). Many children will identify with Gloria, who is truly a different kind of angel. Her hair is tangled, her halo is bent, and her wings are out of shape. She fails miserably at being a proper angel and gets sent to earth. On her way down she crashes into the wall of a barn, hears the cry of a baby, and ends up announcing the birth of God's Son. What's utterly delightful about the story is how Gloria, definitely not a perfect angel, manages to make the greatest of all announcements. Besides the storybook, there are four other supplementary items, available separately: a reflection activity storybook, a poster, a note card, and a stageplay book.

A Christmas book that is an all-time favorite is the classic *A Christmas Carol* by Charles Dickens (DK Publishing, Inc., 1997). Every generation of children has a right to be inspired by Dickens' message—that we can and we should change ourselves and our world for the better.

Remarkably, this edition introduces the reader to the powerful words of the original text. It's an abridgment based on the version Dickens made for his public readings. Included in the book are wonderful illustrations by Andrew Wheatcroft that bring the classic scenes to life. Photography, paintings, and hundreds of facts explore Dickens' London, the wealth and the poverty of the times, and Christmas customs and ideals then and now. This story would be perfect for one of the season's catechetical or religion classes.

A great illustrator and writer of children's books is Brian Wildsmith. One of his most enchanting is *A Christmas Story* (Alfred A. Knopf, Inc., 1980) about a child who helps a young donkey search for his mother. When they find his mother, they also find a newborn baby lying in a manger. The illustrations are exquisite. This is a book to treasure and to look at again and again.

An inspiring Christmas story is *Jacob's Gift* by Max Lucado (Tommy Nelson, 1998). Not only does a rabbi value competence and encourage it in one of his apprentices, he also instructs him that gifts are given to share with others. What Jacob, the young apprentice, does with his woodworking project reveals that he not only learned well his rabbi's teaching, but is deservedly rewarded for his kindness and skill.

Books are great gifts that can enhance and deepen the meaning of Christmas: Jesus, Emmanuel, has come and is with us.

An Often-Told and Much-Loved Story

One time I asked a fifth-grade class to imagine that they were in Bethlehem the night Jesus was born and to write a story of their experience. I was genuinely surprised at the results. Some of them reported that there was something unusual going on in a nearby barn—a lot of activity like shepherds gathering around the place, going in and going out, and acting differently from the way shepherds usually act. One cautioned that shepherds never leave their sheep alone, so that was unusual behavior. All of them alluded to the night darkness but didn't think that was unusual, except for a bright, bright star. None of them saw angels or heard them speaking.

One girl wrote that one of the shepherds was her father, and he told her that he had seen and heard angels in the middle of the night telling them to leave their flocks and go. He and other shepherds went quickly to the stable where a mother was cradling a newborn baby and the father was doing everything to make sure the mother and baby were safe and warm. The shepherd said that there was something special about the baby but he couldn't describe it—he could only feel it. Another child wrote that the birth happened in his neighborhood and they have never stopped talking about it. He said that the stable has been preserved, is on a special town registry, and is frequently visited by the townspeople and other visitors, especially at Christmastime.

The children's stories revealed that the biblical Christmas story is one they know and love. It matters not that in their imaginations there is an ordinariness about the event. Yet all of them expressed a belief that the baby was not an ordinary baby, and one wrote that that baby has changed everything. All of them referred to him by his name, Jesus.

Although the actual birth of Jesus is recorded in only two of the Gospels—Matthew and Luke—the story is told over and over again in children's literature. Following are some versions that I recommend:

The Stone: A Persian Legend of the Magi by Dianne Hofmeyer, illustrated by Jude Daly (Farrar, Straus and Giroux, 1998) is a retelling of an account in the journal of the thirteenth-century Venetian traveler Marco Polo. Three magi of Persia follow a strange star and find a special child.

Peter Collington, author of *A Small Miracle* (Alfred A. Knopf, Inc., 1997), uses not a single word but ninety-six exquisite miniatures to create a contemporary parable. A starving old woman witnesses the vandalizing of the village church. She sells her most prized possession and gives her last ounce of strength to reassembling the Christmas nativity figures before she collapses in the snow. How she is saved is a never-to-be forgotten and profoundly fascinating Christmas tale.

The Miracle of Saint Nicholas by Gloria Whelan (Bethlehem Books/Ignatius Press, 1997) is a story of a small boy in the Russian village of Zeema who asks, among his many other questions, "Why is our church closed?" What he does to reopen the church sets free the amazing and wondrous secrets held over the years by the villagers.

In Robert Byrd's *Saint Francis and the Christmas Donkey* (Dutton Children's Books, a division of Penguin Putnam Books for Young Readers, 2000), St. Francis helps an unhappy donkey appreciate his marvelous origins and teaches him the power of who he really is. The author configures the stories of the creation and of the nativity in a way that addresses the inherent, redeeming good in all of us.

All children's Bibles tell the story of the birth of Jesus and all of them do it well. One that I particularly like is *The Bible: The Really Interesting Bits! Great Events from the Bible,* illustrated by Brian Delf (Tyndale House Publishers, Inc., 1999). The story of Jesus' birth is centrally placed on a two-page spread surrounded by miniature stories and pictures of events that led up to his birth and followed it. The retelling is simply done within a wonderful visual panorama. This book would make a very good family Christmas gift.

To Read Aloud Is the Best Gift of All

Many adults wonder what the best gift is for their children. The answer is to read aloud, but that may seem either too easy or too hard. If either of those "may seems" is yours, a book that will convince you of the "gift" of reading aloud is *Reading Magic: Why Reading Aloud to Our Children Will Change Their Lives Forever* by Mem Fox (Harcourt, Inc., 2001).

In fifteen chapters, the author not only describes the value of reading aloud, but tells how to do it easily and well. I quoted Fox in the Introduction and will repeat her words here. She believes that "if every parent—and every adult caring for a child—were to read aloud a minimum of three stories a day to the children in their lives, we could probably wipe out illiteracy within one generation."

December is a perfect time to read aloud. During the busyness of the season, many children long for the attention and closeness that reading aloud provides. As a gift to yourself, get a copy of Mem Fox's book from a library or bookstore. It's an easy read and even before you've finished it, you can try out the author's reading-aloud suggestions.

The best stories are those that your child wants to hear over and over. You may already have some of those, particularly Christmas stories, on your child's bookshelf. When our goddaughter, Angela, was three, we read to her *The Story of the Three Wise Kings* by Tomie dePaola (G. P. Putnam's Sons, 1983). She couldn't hear it often enough. Gradually, she began reading it aloud to us; however, she always ended *her* version with the words: "Those kings loved that baby so much that they wanted a baby, too."

Here are some other read-aloud recommendations for Christmas:

In *The Miracle of the Myrrh* by Marci Alborghetti, illustrated by Hervé Blondon (Winslow Press, 2000), a grandfather lovingly tells his grandchildren what became of the Little Drummer Boy and the gifts the Wise Men left for the baby Jesus.

In *December* by Eve Bunting (Harcourt Brace, 1997), Simon and his mother are celebrating Christmas Eve in the cardboard house they built themselves. They have a tiny tree but little else. An old woman who has even less asks for shelter and they share what they have. What happens because of their generosity is a "miracle."

The Night of Las Posadas by Tomie dePaola (G. P. Putnam's Sons, 1994) is about the Mexican legend in which the annual Christmas Eve tradition of *Las Posadas* (a festive re-creation of Mary and Joseph's search for an inn) almost doesn't happen until "Jesus and Mary" show up to lead the procession.

In *The Legend of the Poinsettia* by Tomie dePaola (G. P. Putnam's Sons, 1994), when a child is unable to finish her gift for the baby Jesus in time for the Christmas procession, a miracle enables her to offer the beautiful flower we now call the poinsettia.

The Trees of the Dancing Goats by Patricia Polacco (Simon & Schuster, 1996) tells of the generosity and kindness of Jewish neighbors who enable families who are ill and bedridden with scarlet fever to celebrate Christmas.

In *The Story of Christmas,* folk painter Jane Ray (Dutton's Children's Books, 1991) brings the nativity story to life with rich color, drama, and sensitivity.

The Best Christmas Pageant Ever by Barbara Robinson (Harper & Row, 1972) tells about the Herdmans, absolutely the worst kids in the history of the world. Yet their version of the Christmas story makes the annual pageant the best one ever.

In *Tree of Cranes* by Allen Say (Houghton Mifflin, 1991), because of his mother's childhood memory of Christmas in California, a young boy in Japan celebrates his first Christmas.

Chris Van Allsburg, in *The Polar Express* (Houghton Mifflin, 1985), tells of a small boy who, on Christmas Eve, rides a magical train to the North Pole, where he receives a special gift from Santa Claus. A silver bell is a good gift to give as part of this read-aloud.

The Nativity by Julie Vivas (Harcourt Brace, 1988) is a delightful and wondrously illustrated version of the Christmas story.

In *The Sign of the Beaver* by Elizabeth George Speare (Bantam Doubleday Dell, 1984), after twelve-year-old Matt and his father have finished building a cabin for their family in the Maine wilderness, his father leaves him to bring the rest of the family to the new settlement. Matt survives on his own, but worries that they will never return. They do—on Christmas Day! This is one of my favorite December stories. It's also a Newbery Honor book.

4

LENT
AND EASTER

Tales of Grace and Resurrection
Are Easter Stories

In the foreword to An Epidemic of Joy: Stories in the Spirit of Jesus by Andrew Greeley and Mary Greeley Durkin (Acta Publications, 1999), John Shea, theologian and storyteller, says, "Grace is always present, but we seldom see it coming." This, for me, is the ever-present and ongoing story of Easter and resurrection. When the presence of grace takes over, "resurrection"—in many forms—is the outcome.

For example, after my sister's friend of twelve years died when his small plane crashed, she was sure that she couldn't go on without him. The presence of grace was felt in the people who put their arms around my sister and all of us as we wept in disbelief and struggled with the excruciating loss of Ken's presence. Grace, at that time, was the source and harbinger of resurrection.

Recently, one of my nieces, who is disabled, got an unexpected year-end bonus and was told that she's doing a good job.

There's no question that grace has been operative in her work with homebound elderly. The recognition of her success by others creates a resurrection in her that is palpable.

Each vignette in *An Epidemic of Joy* is a grace story revealing the mystery of resurrection. Some of the stories help us to see what happens when people relate in healthy and unhealthy ways; others help us to see ourselves in the behaviors of others; many remind us that unconditional loving is God's way with us; and all of them put us in touch with the spirit of Jesus.

Reading these stories once is not enough. Repeat readings awaken something new each time, which is what resurrection does—it keeps renewing us.

Because "grace" and "resurrection" are so much a part of the human story, it's not surprising that authors of children's literature use those threads to weave their tales. Here are some that I recommend:

In *Sophie* by Mem Fox, illustrated by Aminah Brenda Lynn Robinson (Harcourt Brace and Company, 1994), Sophie and her grandpa love each other. Their lives enrich and give joy to each other as Sophie grows from an infant to adult and Grandpa grows older and older. They are always there for each other until Grandpa dies and there is no Grandpa—just emptiness and sadness for a while until new life when a tiny hand holds on to Sophie and sweetness fills the world once again.

Mama by Eleanor Schick (Marshall Cavendish, 2000) recounts the memories of a little girl from the moment Mama tells her that she is sick. The girl remembers the things they did together and the things Mama said during her illness. The girl remembers, too, how she cried and cried when Papa told her that Mama had died, and how she felt as if she was "spinning off the edge of the world." Louise, a woman who comes to stay after Mama's death, holds her and rocks her and keeps assuring her,

"It's going to be alright, child." She also helps her to believe that Mama didn't leave her but remains in her heart and will always be with her. Gradually, the little girl's remembering helps her to cope and to incorporate her mother's wisdom and presence into her everyday life.

Yolanda's Genius by Carol Fenner (Aladdin Paperbacks, 1997) is an award-winning tale of a widowed mother who moves her family out of Chicago to a safer place after six-year-old Andrew shows her a packet of cocaine that someone has given him. The small town is different for eleven-year-old Yolanda and is safer, except for an incident in which Andrew is hustled by some older kids who destroy his harmonica and silence his gift for making the instrument speak.

Yolanda feels responsible for Andrew's losses because she was supposed to take care of him and didn't. From then on she is determined to restore to Andrew both the instrument and his genius for making music with sounds he hears and images he sees—and also to convince the world, and especially their mother, of Andrew's gift.

I hope that this small sampling of grace and resurrection stories will whet your appetite and encourage you to read.

Books Have the Power to Change Lives

Lent is a time of hope. Winter is winding down. The light of longer days overcomes darkness. Crocuses appear suddenly. The season itself calls for a change in behavior. We're challenged to put on a new self.

Lent is also a perfect time to ponder, reflect on, and address issues that affect the children in our lives, the broader community, and the world. A book for adults that can help us do that is *Tikvah:*

Children's Book Creators Reflect on Human Rights (Seastar Books, 1999). Forty-four of the best authors and illustrators of children's literature use words and pictures to explore subjects ranging from child labor to racial integration to religious freedom. Their hope is to foster a kinder, more tolerant world. In the introduction, Elie Wiesel says, "*Tikvah* means hope and hope is represented by children. It is they who must justify our hope in education, human relations, and social justice. In other words: they represent our hope in a future which is an improvement on our past."

Tikvah is a powerful book because, first, it's beautiful and second, it represents these artists' firm commitment to human rights. Their visions of hope can inspire each of us to become more committed to the importance of respecting the rights of others and of the basic social connections that we all share. I hope that everyone will pick it up and savor it, and even buy copies to give as gifts.

In the Foreword to *Tikvah* we're reminded that books have the power to change lives. Here are some that could do that:

One Candle by Eve Bunting (Joanna Cotler Books, an imprint of HarperCollins Publishers, 2002) tells of one family's traditional Hanukkah celebration, in which a special story is retold every year and passed on to each generation by Grandma and Great-Aunt Rose. It's a touching and joyous tale about the importance of remembrance.

Let There Be Light by Jane Breskin Zalbin (Dutton Children's Books, 2002) is an unusual collection of "Poems and Prayers for Repairing the World." Some of the poems and prayers are familiar; others are new and different. In the dedication, the author says, "I pray our family continues to grow through love, and, with it, the world."

The Nightingale by Stephen Mitchell (Candlewick Press, 2002) is a retelling of Hans Christian Andersen's beloved story, which he wrote in 1844. The emperor of China lives in the most marvelous palace, but lovelier than all, say visitors to his realm, is the song of the nightingale in the forest by the sea. When the emperor learns of the nightingale, he has to have it, and when it is brought to the palace, he is enchanted by the bird's sweet song. But when a mechanical bird is brought into the palace, the nightingale flies back to her green forest. Eventually the mechanism in the mechanical bird gives out, the emperor falls seriously ill, and the nightingale returns in time to save him from death.

This story does well what Bruno Bettelheim says of fairy tales: they offer reassurance; they provide ways to find meaning and to sort out difficulties; and they offer hope.

Seeds of hope are planted in children's lives when their homes are places of peace and comfort and their families provide them with support and guidance and share stories with them. That is why William Bennett compiled a beautifully illustrated anthology titled *The Children's Book of Home and Family* (Random House Children's Books, 2002). All the selections in the book center around family life. The author believes that these kinds of stories and poetry provide a good way for adults and children to talk about beliefs they hold dear.

If none of the above titles is available, go to your local library or children's bookstore and read selections until you find one or two that you like and that will capture your children's imaginations and be helpful in their own stories.

Stories for the Lenten Season

"What's done is done!" This fatalistic attitude is one I've sometimes entertained after making a mess of things. Since the attitude is mostly unproductive, I usually pull myself together and find a way to rectify or change what has happened, hopefully to bring about some redemption or resurrection.

Lent is a time for *soul-searching*, a time to admit that we frequently make a mess of things, that we're frequently less than we might be. It's a perfect time to take a long look at our interior landscape to discover what's messy there; it's a time for spiritual renewal, a time to put into gear an inner can-do, can-change attitude. It's a time to deal with the fragments of evil that show up in our behavior and cast shadows over our own happiness and the happiness of others in our families, communities, and society.

Because transformation is so clear in fairy and folk tales, I return to them for Lenten reading and inspiration. And I always use them as part of my Lenten classes.

My favorite is *The Selfish Giant* by Oscar Wilde (Simon and Schuster Books for Young Readers, 1984). What happens in the giant's garden can be likened to the effects of evil and goodness in our hearts and spirits. In this version the appearance, disappearance, and reappearance of the child simply and gently puts the reader in touch with death, new life, death, and the promises of new life.

Another is *The Seven Ravens* by the Brothers Grimm. This story shows up in all of the major collections of Grimm's fairy tales, but a version I particularly like is the adaptation by Laura Geringer (HarperCollins, 1994). A small child uses her powers of courage, faith in forgiveness, and love to undo the evil that her father unwittingly, in anger, brought down on her brothers.

A tale that gives both pain and pleasure to the spirit is *The Mightiest Heart* by Lynn Cullen (Dial Books, 1998). It is a story of faithfulness and salvation, regret and sorrow, and a promise of new life and hope. This tale helps capture the truth that sometimes missteps are serious ones that can't be undone, but mysteriously and graciously, second chances are given.

The Tale of the Three Trees retold by Angela Ewell Hunt (Lion Publishing, 1989) is a near-perfect, startlingly simple story of the transformation of trees into objects that hold Jesus at key moments in his life—a manger for his birth, a boat in which to calm a storm, and a cross to reveal that he is, indeed, God's son.

Another tale, one that is a mysterious description of the change that can occur if we really enter into the call and challenges of the Lenten season, is *Through the Mickle Woods* by Valiska Gregory (Little, Brown & Company, 1992). The queen dies and the king loses heart. He has little desire to continue living. Michael, a small boy, convinces the king to open a box from the queen. In it are a ring and a letter sealed with wax. The letter asks the king to do one more thing for her: to go forth into the Mickle Woods to find the bear. She also says that the child will give the ring to the bear. The king resists, but because it is the queen's wish, he agrees to go with Michael. The journey is hard, but they arrive in the Mickle Woods and are greeted by the bear, who tells them three stories. As each story is told, Michael and the king remember what the queen was like and what she loved. This enables the king to let go of his loss, to feel new life and hope, and to go on living again.

Besides single folk and fairy tale titles, there are many collections. If you use a collection, choose stories from it that touch your heart and spirit and in which you find meaning and sustenance. Because there are many layers of meaning in these tales, I suggest that you refrain from telling children what meanings the stories may contain. The enrichment that occurs in each child's spiritual life from reading or hearing a tale will differ from yours and from that of other children.

To get the most out of these stories, I suggest *Fairy Tales, Fables, Legends, and Myths: Using Folk Literature in Your Classroom* by Betty Bosma (Teacher's College Press, 1987).

Stories of Chaos and Darkness: A Lenten Resource

Recently, in a medical center, I rode on an elevator with a young man who was leaning heavily against the back wall. Spontaneously, I asked, "Are you okay?" He held up what looked like "orders" and answered, "No, I'm terrified!" As we left the elevator, he asked me if I knew how to get to radiology. I directed him to the department and wished him luck. He smiled wanly and we parted. I keep thinking about him and praying that his body will heal and that his spirit will find peace.

Lent is like what the young man was experiencing—a time of reckoning with chaos and darkness. The question is, "How do we push through it to hope?"

A book that can help us accept the truth that chaos happens is *This Blessed Mess: Finding Hope Amidst Life's Chaos* by Patricia H. Livingston (Sorin Books, 2000). Livingston believes that chaos is simply another name for energy and power, untamed and unformed, but not bad. Her book is full of personal stories of chaos and how she tamed it with hope and courage.

Children, too, experience chaos. Stories are a great resource for helping them to name it and to hold on to hope. Here are some to consider:

In *Grandma's Purple Flowers* by Adjoa J. Burrowes (Lee & Low, 2000), a young child loves her grandmother and visits her all the time. Along the way she picks purple flowers. A big hug and a smile are always waiting, and when Grandma sees the purple flowers her smile grows wide. During the visits they do special things together that make both of them happy.

One winter day Grandma is not herself, and that night she dies. All winter the young girl misses her grandmother terribly.

But with time and the arrival of spring, she finds a way to cope and discovers her own special way to remember Grandma.

In *The Brand New Kid* by Katie Couric (Doubleday, 2000), Lazlo S. Gasky is in a new school. The other kids see him as different and treat him badly. He gradually gives up on trying to fit in and simply prepares for the next taunt and tease.

One day when Lazlo's mother comes to pick him up, Ellie, a classmate, notices her sadness and finds out from a friend that she is worried that the school may be wrong for her son and she may have to pull him out. Ellie decides to do something and invites Lazlo to play at her house or his. They become friends, and, following Ellie's lead, the other children also befriend him.

Allison by Allen Say (Houghton Mifflin, 1997) tells about a small child who realizes that she looks different from her mother and father and decides that they aren't her parents. She deals with her adoption destructively until she is prompted to give attention to a stray cat. When she wants to adopt the cat, her parents let her after she assures them that the cat will be happy in their family.

In *Tikvah Means Hope* by Patricia Polacco (Doubleday, 1994), following a devastating firestorm a small group of people gather in a Sukkah that mysteriously is not destroyed. But their hearts are so sad they can't celebrate until Tikvah, a missing cat, emerges. They believe it's a miracle and they begin to hope again.

In *Gathering Blue* by Lois Lowry (Houghton Mifflin, 2000), Kira is orphaned and flawed in a civilization that shuns and discards the weak. She finds herself facing the Council of Guardians, who will decide if she is to live or die. Because Kira possesses a gift that the community needs, the council's judgment is positive. All of her needs are taken care of under the protection of the council, yet Kira struggles with the mysteries and questions in her life. On her quest for truth, she makes painful discoveries and, although she could have chosen otherwise, she unselfishly chooses what is best for her community.

Learning that chaos and darkness open up new life can help children understand Lent as a preparation for Easter.

Good Lenten Reading: Books That Build Character

One of the best things I did during my years of teaching in parochial schools is read stories aloud for fifteen minutes every day. Occasionally, I've met again some of my former students, now adults. None of them remarked about how good I was at teaching English (which I was), or how poor at teaching math (which was also true). All of them remembered one or more of the stories I had read, why they liked them so much, and what they meant to them then and even now.

One of my students told me that when I'd start a story, she and her mother would get it from the library and would read it together but would never go ahead of where we were in school. She said that she loved hearing each chapter for the first time in school and then again at home. Two students told me that they have read aloud some of the same stories to their own children, and one has become the "storybook lady" at a local library.

In "Imagination: The Heart's Best Guide," the first chapter of *Books That Build Character* by William Kilpatrick and Gregory and Suzanne M. Wolfe (Touchstone, 1994), the authors cite a 1985 report by the National Commission on Reading that declares that reading aloud is the single most important contribution parents can make toward their child's success in school. The authors add that reading aloud may also be one of the most important contributions parents can make toward developing good character in their children:

> First, because stories can create an emotional attachment to goodness, a desire to do the right thing. Second, because stories provide a wealth of good examples—the kind of examples that are often missing from a child's day-to-day environment. Third, because stories familiarize children with the codes of conduct they need to know. Finally, because stories help to make sense out of life, help us to cast our own lives as stories. Unless this sense of meaning is acquired at an early age and reinforced as we grow older, there simply is no moral growth.

Since catechists hope to strengthen in the young their moral sense, it seems wise and good to make a habit of reading aloud stories that build character. This is possible in lessons that are as short as twenty or thirty minutes, certainly in those that are longer. I personally read aloud a story in every class—one that fits and enhances a lesson's message.

Story is a way in which children can share in the lives of people who unselfishly sacrifice for others, who are honest and truthful in spite of consequences, who are brave and courageous in heroic ways. From stories, children can also learn that struggles and suffering have meaning, that there is always reason to hope.

I strongly recommend *Books That Build Character* because of the case it builds for using stories to teach moral values and also for its book list, which is accompanied by descriptions of how each title engages the moral imagination.

Here are some that I've used with children and recommend:

The Clown of God by Tomie dePaola (Harcourt Brace Jovanovich, 1978), a story about a juggler, can enhance a child's belief that he or she has something to offer that can be the basis for hope and future achievement. An exquisite version of the legend this story is based on is *The Acrobat and the Angel* by Mark and David Shannon (G. P. Putnam's Sons, 1999).

In *The Jade Stone* by Caryn Yacowitz (Holiday House, 1992), Chan Lo, a stone carver, disobeys the Great Emperor of all China in spite of his fear of punishment, because he can't go against what he knows he has to do.

In *The Paper Crane* by Molly Bang (Mulberry Books, 1987), when a new highway replaces an old road, a busy roadside diner ends up with few customers. One day a poor, ragged stranger appears. He is fed generously and treated as though he were a king. The stranger rewards the kindness of the restaurant owner with a magical gift.

The Children's Book of Heroes by William J. Bennett (Simon & Schuster, 1997) helps children to know what kindness and compassion look like.

Resurrection Happens All the Time

After a few weeks of Lent, some of us find our minds and imaginations entertaining thoughts of resurrection. This happened to me, in a profound way, following a reading of *Ordinary Resurrections* by Jonathan Kozol (Crown Publishers, 2000). Rarely do I fall head over heels in love with a book, its reflections and observations, as I did with this one.

I savored the way the author revealed life through the eyes of children in New York's South Bronx, with whom he had spent time and whom he grew to love over a period of seven years. The delightful, almost poetic way in which he writes about his encounters with the children and the adults in their lives fascinated and inspired me. For example, he says of the Caribbean lilt of Katrice, a woman who is a constant in the children's lives, "I'm reminded of imaginary music." And in describing the parents as "recognizing the outer limits of the opportunities that this society is giving their children," he added that "they also know the limits of the opportunities that they can offer to their children; and they know these aren't the same as what another class of people in another section of the city are providing for their children. So they look at their sons and daughters with this secret piece of knowledge. They know how destinies are formed out of particulars."

The children in this book struggle with daily challenges and disadvantages that many children in America neither experience nor even imagine. Many parents are also unaware of the great inequities that exist. That's the heartbreaking underlying story, and it's why reading this book is vital to appreciating that equality and justice are, in truth, not enjoyed by all and that many children and families are victims.

The primary power of this book lies in how the author shows that these children (and I suspect most children) cannot be easily categorized, that surviving is what these children do every day, and that somehow in the mystery of it all there are frequent flashes of Easter.

In children's literature the landscape is covered with ordinary resurrections. Flashes of Easter regularly happen, and the ways in which many fictional children live out the details of their lives are inspiring. I will identify only two such stories.

A particularly special one is *Nory Ryan's Song* by Patricia Reilly Giff (Delacorte Press, 2000). Nory lives in Ireland with her family under an English government that is not only indifferent but also cruel. When the potato famine hits, most Irish cannot pay their rent and food is so scarce that more than a million people die of starvation and illness. Yet at the same time, more than enough food to feed Ireland's population is being exported across the sea.

The suffering that Nory and her family and the broader community experience is so painful that I couldn't keep from crying at times while I read the story. Yet I kept holding on to slivers of hope from the ordinary resurrections that occurred each time a bit of food was scrounged, each time comfort was provided (in Nory's case, by an elderly woman named Anna), each time something unexpected happened (like finding a drawing that her sister, Maggie, had sent from New York). Finally the ticket arrived that enabled Nory to join her family in America.

Another book is *The Gardener* by Sarah Stewart (Farrar, Straus and Giroux, 1997). Lydia Grace's father has been out of work for a long time, and no one asks her mother to make dresses anymore. Her Uncle Jim, a baker, invites her to live with him in the city until things get better. Lydia Grace knows nothing about baking but a lot about gardening. She does learn about baking, but she also creatively seizes upon every opportunity to plant seeds and bulbs. Finally, with a hope to get her Uncle Jim to smile, she plants a secret garden. There is more than one resurrection at the end of the story: Lydia Grace's secret garden blooms, her uncle surprises her with an amazing cake covered with flowers, her father gets a job, and Lydia Grace goes home.

The more you read children's literature, the more you will be sensitive to the truth that "resurrection does not wait for Easter."

Death-to-Resurrection Stories and Newbery Award Winners

Recently I gave a workshop to parents and teachers who were preparing young teens for the sacrament of confirmation.

The participants asked many tough questions: "Who are these teens?" "What are they like?" "How do they deal with stuff?" and "How can you find out what's going on in them?"

There's a wealth of information in professional books and videos that explore these life questions. Living and working with preteens and young teens can also provide some answers. A great resource for "in-depth answers" is literature written for and about them.

Surprisingly, some of the best children's literature is written for those ages. What is also of great note, and germane to the Easter season, is that the journey from death to resurrection is profoundly present in much of it. Most winners of the coveted Newbery Medal are writers who, with great skill, tell the story of their characters through the death-resurrection prism. I doubt that they do it with conscious intent, yet it consistently happens. I consider many of these books grace-filled gifts.

A perfect example is *Holes* by Louis Sachar (Farrar, Straus and Giroux, 1998; National Book Award, 1998; Newbery, 1999). Stanley is a young boy whose family has a history of bad luck. Through a miscarriage of justice, he is sent to Camp Green Lake, a boys' juvenile detention center. There is no lake; it's been dry for over a hundred years. Each boy has to dig a hole a day, five feet deep, five feet across in the hard, unforgiving, sunbaked earth. There is a hidden agenda, but the warden claims that digging these holes builds character. It's hot, the digging is beyond hard, and survival is a painful, game-playing challenge. As the story progresses, Stanley overcomes each challenge, digs up the truth, and brings about redemption for himself, for another boy encamped with him, and for his family.

The Door in the Wall by Marguerite de Angeli (Bantam Doubleday Dell Books for Young Readers, 1990; Newbery, 1950) is set in medieval England. It's about a young boy named Robin, the son of a nobleman, whose destiny is changed suddenly when he falls ill and loses the use of his legs. His parents, unaware of his plight, are in the service of the king and queen and he is alone in the midst of a plague. A monk named Brother Luke rescues him, and under his care Robin learns many things, especially patience and courage. He eventually joins his godfather, Sir Peter, at the great castle of Lindsay. When the castle and the townspeople are endangered, Robin, with ingenuity and great courage, saves them. In this story resurrections happen over and over again.

Summer, the young protagonist in *Missing May* by Cynthia Rylant (Orchard Books, 1992; Newbery, 1993), is twelve when Aunt May dies. Although Summer's grief is profound, it is Uncle Ob who seems unable to go on living without his beloved companion. With the help of one of her schoolmates, Summer and Uncle Ob go on a journey in search of healing at the Spiritualist Church of Glen Meadow. Their quest seems doomed when they learn that the preacher they hoped to meet died several months earlier. All seems lost until, on the return journey, something happens to Uncle Ob. As if in answer to Summer's silent prayers, he chooses life over mourning. It's a powerful story of internal rather than external changes.

In *Call It Courage* by Armstrong Sperry (Aladdin Books, 1990; Newbery, 1991), a young boy overcomes fear and does what he has to do to gain respect.

Lois Lowry's *The Giver* (Houghton Mifflin, 1993; Newbery, 1994) is described as a fascinating, thoughtful, science fiction novel. It takes place in a nameless community, at an unidentified future time. The life is utopian: There is no hunger, no disease, no pollution, no fear; old age is tenderly cared for; every child has concerned and attentive parents. Every aspect of life has a prescribed rule.

Young Jonas is eagerly awaiting the Ceremony of Twelve, the time when all twelve-year-olds in the community receive their assignments for their lifelong professions. He is astonished when he is selected to be trained to be the new Receiver of Memories, the most respected of the leaders. What he learns in his training, he finds horrifying. How he deals with what he learns is a courageous personal triumph and the beginning of new life.

Summer might be an ideal time for parents and teachers to borrow Newbery books from their local libraries to read alone or with their young teens. This may be, for some, an unrealistic recommendation. However, I know teachers who read a "kid's book" a week during the summer and parents who started reading children's books on a family vacation and got "hooked."

Listings of Newbery Medal Books are available for free in most libraries and are also online at the Website of the American Library Association, the organization that awards the medal. Go to www.ala.org, then enter "Newbery" into the site search engine.

Story Can Help Children Reflect on Death and Resurrection

Easter, with its burst of new life, is the greatest of all Christian feasts. It's the glorious outcome of Christ's story, which included agony, pain, acceptance, forgiveness, death, and finally, resurrection.

The truth and wonder of the Easter event are embedded in our spirits. What happened at Easter is so rooted in who we are that it both perceptibly and imperceptibly shapes who we are now and who we are becoming. It's also a yardstick for measuring and reckoning with the life-changing events in our own stories.

Oftentimes we measure and reckon after such an event rather than during it. That is what Carl and I did with an event that engulfed us one summer. My ninety-six-year-old mother had been living alone in her own home, doing reasonably well. But my three brothers, my sister, and I were concerned about her living alone through another Iowa winter with its snow, ice, and freezing cold. The decision for her to go to a retirement complex took place during one of our visits home. We thought she had precipitated the decision. She decided that we had, and the anger she felt was directed at us. We found ourselves returning to Iowa again and again to be with her as she dealt with the agony of going through forty-one years of cherished possessions. She would have done anything rather than what we, as a family, were forcing her to do. As she gave up many of her precious things and left her beloved home, we all experienced dying in a way that none of us had experienced before. And, unlike the three days in between Jesus' death and resurrection, my mother's "resurrection" to a new life took longer, but gradually it happened. Mysteriously, she is a new person in many ways. Her resurrection has also changed us.

Dying and rising happen not only in adults but in children as well. Anyone who has experienced with children divorce, death, the loss of a friend or pet, abandonment, illness, a move away from school and friends, homelessness, or the imprisonment of a family member appreciates the rhythm of death and resurrection in their stories. This movement can help children to ride out their personal storms and trust that things will get better. Story can help children to remember that there is more to the picture than what they have recently been seeing and feeling. It can also help them be less scared about death.

A reflective and gentle story that does some of the above is *The Collector of Moments* by Quint Buchholz (Farrar, Straus and

Giroux, 1999). A solitary boy spends days in Max's studio, and each evening at dusk he plays his violin. Sometimes the artist sings along, sometimes he's just silent. But no matter how much time the boy spends in the studio, he is never allowed to see the paintings until the artist goes on a journey. He leaves behind a surprise exhibition for the boy. The boy studies each of the pictures and discovers answers to all his questions.

After the boy has spent time pondering each of the paintings, the artist returns to get his things and to move on. Before he leaves, he tells the boy that he is a very special person and, by all means, he should continue to make music. The boy misses his friend until one day a box arrives from the artist with a new picture and a message. He tells the boy that his music is always there in his pictures. This gives the boy a sense of his continued connection with the artist and helps him accept his own gift, so that he eventually uses it to inspire and teach others.

The Heavenly Village by Cynthia Rylant (Scholastic, Inc., 1999) is an unusually playful and imaginative story that deals with the mystery of life after death. Since no one knows what happens after death, stories about people living happily and productively in a stopping place between heaven and earth seem plausible and comforting. Rylant is one of the best authors of children's literature and, like her other works, this one is both powerful and beautiful. Reading this kind of story can feed hungers that are hidden in our hearts and minds and can build bridges between reality and mystery.

5

RESOURCES FOR
THE MIND AND SPIRIT

Summertime Is Good Reading Time

Summer is a good time to dip deeply into children's literature and to read aloud to children as well as to read silently to yourself. To help ease you into this, I recommend Jim Trelease's revised edition of his *Read-Aloud Handbook* (Penguin Books, 2001). It's unquestionably the best book on stories and reading them aloud that I've found. Besides encouraging and inspiring us to read, Trelease also deepens our sense of the value of story in children's and young people's lives. He believes that the breadth and depth of our knowledge of books are an important part of successfully bringing children and books together. To support this belief he supplies a comprehensive catalogue of titles that he calls a treasury, in which he lists "Picture Books," "Short Novels," "Full-Length Novels," "Poetry," and "Anthologies." In many instances, he indicates the appropriate age level and gives a brief description of the work.

While too recent to be named in Trelease's treasury, these titles are good for your summer reading list:

A *Single Shard* by Linda Sue Park (Clarion Books, 2001) is about Tree Ear, an orphan living under a bridge in twelfth-century Korea who becomes fascinated with a nearby community of potters. The book won the Newbery Medal. Kathleen Odean, who heads the Newbery Award Committee, said of it: "Tree Ear's determination and bravery in pursuing his dream of becoming a potter takes readers on a literary journey that demonstrates how courage, honor, and perseverance can overcome great odds and bring great happiness."

Another remarkable and timely tale is *The Breadwinner* by Deborah Ellis (Groundwood Books/Douglas & McIntyre, 2000). This story takes place in Afghanistan under the Taliban, whose extreme religious views include forbidding women to appear in public without being covered from head to toe. They can't go to school, work outside the home, or leave their homes without a man to escort them. The heroine of the story is eleven-year-old Parvana, who lives with her family in one room of a bombed-out apartment building. After her father is arrested for having a foreign education, the family is left without someone who can earn money or even shop for food. As conditions for the family grow desperate, only one solution emerges. Parvana must transform herself into a boy and become the breadwinner.

Two stories that give a powerful and painful glimpse of what life was like for slaves during their flight to freedom are Shelley Pearsall's *Trouble Don't Last* (Alfred A. Knopf, 2002) and Deborah Hopkinson's *Under the Quilt of Night* (Atheneum Books for Young Readers, 2001). In *Trouble Don't* Last eleven-year-old Samuel is pulled from his bed without warning one dark night by cranky old Harrison, a fellow slave, and together they run. It's a heartbreaking and hopeful novel of the Underground Railroad, freedom, and family.

Under the Quilt of Night is a poetic tale of a slave girl who starts to run. She follows the moon into the woods, leading her loved ones away from their master. There's only one place where he may not find them and it's under the quilt of night. With the stars as a guide, she comes upon a cloth quilt with a center square made from deep blue fabric. She recognizes it as a signal from friends on the Underground Railroad who welcome her into their home and help her and her loved ones to freedom. The art by James E. Ransome that accompanies the words in this book is hauntingly and memorably beautiful.

Juan Verdades by Joe Hayes (Orchard Books, 2001) is an amazing story of a man who couldn't tell a lie. It's not a version of our George Washington story; rather, it's a tale of a man who is severely tested but manages to triumph by telling the truth in a unique yet authentic way. This story fits all ages.

As part of your summertime reading you might browse in local bookstores. Check, too, for recommendations in the book section of Sunday editions of your local newspaper. The more you read children's literature, the more you'll learn what children are like, how they think, how they deal with adversity, and how they make their way in the world.

More Summer Choices

When I read *Religious Education and the Brain* by Jerry Larsen (Paulist Press, 2000), I knew that I would be recommending it for summer reading. The book truly lives up to the claim of its subtitle—*A Practical Resource for Understanding How We Learn about God*. What I find most significant and helpful about it is the way it deals with how children learn, identifying the brain as a place where meaning develops and is owned. Actually, it identifies the brain as "The Meaning Factory" (chapter 2) and the role of the religious educator as "Factory Consultant" (chapter 3). While I found chapter 3 the most helpful of the twelve chapters, all of them contributed mightily to my understanding and appreciation of how we come to God-sense. I've actually read the book twice and probably will read it again before a new school year begins.

Besides reading a good professional book during the summer, you should also take time to read some examples of children's literature, especially those honored as the best—the Newbery Award winners.

Here are three special stories that you'll remember long after you've read them:

When Marian Sang by Pam Munoz Ryan (Scholastic Press, 2002) is a thoughtful, almost painful introduction to the life of Marian Anderson, one of our country's greatest singers. She is best known for her historic concert on the steps of the Lincoln Memorial in 1939, which drew an integrated crowd of 75,000 people in pre–Civil Rights America. The greatness of her voice will certainly be remembered, but what is even more inspiring is her strength of character while struggling through the times in which she lived.

Inspired by the life of the author's grandmother, *Ruby's Wish* by Shirin Yim Bridges (Chronicle Books, 2002) is an engaging portrait of a determined young girl and a family who rewards her independent spirit.

In Ed Young's *What About Me?* (Philomel Books, 2002), a young boy goes on a quest for knowledge. Everyone he asks for help asks him to fill a need *they* have before they will help him. After he has taken care of everyone else's needs, he surprisingly discovers that he already possesses the knowledge he's searching for.

The Newbery Award stories are so good that they lodge themselves in our memories and spirits and enhance our very being. Another medal winner I strongly recommend:

E. L. Konigsburg's *The View from Saturday* (Atheneum Books, 1996) is a story of a teacher who returns to the classroom after having been injured in an automobile accident. Her sixth-grade Academic Bowl team turns out to be the best and becomes her answer to regaining confidence and success. This is an amazing tale of a teacher, a team, a class, a school, and a series of contests.

In many bookstores, award-winning books are identified and placed together for easy selection. In libraries, they are often listed on fliers along with the dates on which the awards were given. This might be a good way to become familiar with these books and to read as many of them as you can.

Prayer Books for Children and Teens

While I was in Belize, Central America, during Christmastime 2002, I came across an article in the local newspaper titled "Faith and Prayer." The article highlighted the effects of spirituality in people who attend religious services regularly; for example, they tend to experience greater marital satisfaction, alleviation of chronic pain, and less anxiety and stress. The article also refers to Herbert Benson, MD, of Harvard's Mind/Body Institute, who has found that praying for ten to twenty minutes a day can decrease blood pressure, heart rate, breathing, and metabolic rates.

Marianne Williamson, an author and lecturer, is also quoted. She cautions that spirituality is not a substitute for medicine but that "they should work together in the fight against illness." She also says that the most important thing you can do for someone who is ill is to pray for them and ask others to pray. "Prayer is a conduit for miracles," she adds. "It has no harmful side effects, costs nothing, and is proven to work."

More and more people are recognizing the power of prayer because of experiences in which they've found peace, healing, and/or acceptance of the challenges in their lives. I, too, have had an experience recently that gives me a deeper belief in what can happen when we pray.

A young man I've known since he was a child was facing felony charges and the possibility of prison. His lawyer told him that it didn't look good. I couldn't bear the thought that he might be jailed and have a felony on his record. Prior to his scheduled hearing, I decided to pray for him several times a day. I directed my prayers to the Spirit for the judge presiding over the case. For two weeks I didn't let up—I was certain in my belief that prayer could make a difference. It did! The charge was reduced to a misdemeanor, no jail time, community service, or remuneration for damages. I'm aware that there were other mitigating factors, but I haven't the slightest doubt that my praying added mightily to the outcome.

Knowing that prayer is a vital element in our lives makes it imperative that we pray often with our children and young people. Too frequently I've heard catechists and religion teachers say that they have so much to cover in their classes that they don't have time to pray. I'm aware that praying with children and teens is not the sole responsibility of catechists and religion teachers, but children need to experience prayer in their classes as well as at home and within the faith community.

The need for prayer is apparent in the many children's books of prayer that are now available. Here are some of the best:

The prayers in Marian Wright Edelman's collection *I'm Your Child, God: Prayers for Our Children* (Hyperion Books, 2002) embrace issues faced by children and teens in an increasingly complicated world.

The Lord's Prayer by Lois Rock (Paulist Press, 1999) is a beautifully illustrated and reflective prayer guide to the "Our Father."

In John Marsden's book for young and old, *Prayers for the Twenty-First Century* (Star Bright Books, 1998), deeply held hopes and common fears are given visual and prayerful expression.

Intended for use with children in first through fifth grades, *Bless This Day* by Patricia Mathson (Ave Maria Press, 2002) contains 150 prayers that speak to children's experience of God.

Chatter with the Angels by Linda S. Richer and Anita Stoltzfus (GIA Publications, 2000), an illustrated song book, is for use with children ages three to ten. It introduces them to Christian songs that are enjoyable, meaningful, and enduring.

Each of the two books by Patty McCulloch, MHSH, *Encountering Jesus* and *Touching Jesus* (Ave Maria Press, 2001), contains twenty guided meditations on Jesus' care and compassion. The author has used them successfully with both teens and adults.

Joan Bel Geddes wrote *Children Praying* (Sorin Books, 1999) primarily for parents to advise them why and how to pray with children. The insights in it are also valuable for catechists and religion teachers.

A Child's Book of Celtic Prayers, written and compiled by Joyce Denham (Loyola Press, 1998), introduces children to Celtic Christians and their deep belief that God was present wherever they were and in all that they did, as well as in the rest of creation.

It's also good to pray with children in ways that are memorable and fun. *The Rhyme Bible Prayer Book* by L. J. Sattgast

(Zondervan, 2002) is a delightful book of prayers that tap into a child's love of rhyme. It contains morning prayers, evening prayers, and prayers for in-between. Children find the prayers easy to memorize and are delightfully surprised when they spontaneously connect what they see in an illustration to a Bible story they've heard.

Stories of Loss Help Us Cope and Hope

After reading *Lost and Found: A Kid's Book for Living through Loss* by Rabbi Marc Gellman and Monsignor Thomas Hartman (Morrow Junior Books, 1999), I realized that the book might be titled *Death and Resurrection*. The key virtue in the book is hope, and the primary message is that loss, which robs us of something or someone, gives us back something new or something that replaces. In the authors' own words, "Every time something is lost, something can be found."

A large part of the book is about death: it's forever, it comes to everyone, it has steps of sadness, and time is a healer. It also describes kinds of death and, through examples, those who are lost through death.

Other chapters deal with divorce as well as the loss of material goods, games, health, a part of the body, and confidence. A special part of the book is the bibliography of nonfiction and fiction titles. Although written for kids, adults can find in it much that is instructive, meaningful, and helpful.

If you've shared in a child's pain during one or more losses, you may be keenly aware of the importance of the nurture that comes through reading about losses and living vicariously through them with another. Sheldon Kopp, in the introduction to his book *If You Meet the Buddha on the Road, Kill Him!*, wrote,

"As a child, I was so often lonely and out of it that if I had not found the tales of others in the books I read, I believe I would have died."

Other than those books listed in Gellman and Hartman's bibliography, I also recommend the following, which I've used in catechetical sessions with children and/or have suggested to parents for their children's libraries.

In *The Legend of the Persian Carpet* by Tomie dePaola (G. P. Putnam's Sons, 1993), a precious diamond, loved by a king and his people, is stolen from the palace. When the sun had reflected through the diamond, the rooms were filled with a million rainbows of light and color. Without the diamond, they were filled with shadows and gloom. The king was devastated until a small boy found a way to bring the colors back to the room and the king back to his people. It's a perfect tale of treasure lost and treasure regained.

Erandi's Braids is another of dePaola's books (G. P. Putnam's Sons, 1999). When her mother's hair is not long enough, Erandi, a small girl, sells her own thick, beautiful braids. This saddens her mother but makes it possible for them to buy a much-needed fishing net. Erandi's generosity is rewarded when there's enough money left over to buy a much-wanted doll.

Caroline Binch's *Since Dad Left* (Millbrook Press, 1998) is a story about a child who reluctantly learns to deal with his parents' separation and his father's new lifestyle. The pain and anger he feels are palpable. Children of separated and divorced parents will readily identify with Sid's feelings and may find comfort and support in his gradual acceptance of a situation he can't change.

The above are short stories that are easily read in a single session. A longer story is Karen Hesse's *Phoenix Rising* (Puffin Books, 1995). Nyle lives peacefully on a farm with her grandmother until an accident occurs at a nuclear power plant. When her grandmother chooses to take in two of the evacuees, both very ill from radiation sickness, it becomes a major challenge for Nyle. Her grandmother's counsel, "I know you'd rather not get involved in this mess, Nyle, but sometimes you have to do things you'd rather not," helps her do what she needs to do. And in the end, she understands love and hope that rises like a phoenix from destruction and despair.

Stories Nurture the Spirit and Connect Us with the Hero Within

Stories have the power to awaken the truth of the possible in us and can inspire us to strive for it, no matter how hard, daunting, or painful the process may be. They help us to be heroes and heroines. This kind of story abounds in children's literature because it provides the spiritual, psychological, and emotional nurture that children and young people yearn for and willingly read.

One prime example is *Harry Potter and the Sorcerer's Stone* by J. K. Rowlings (Scholastic Press, 1998). Since their publication in the United States, the Harry Potter volumes have sold millions of copies and appear regularly on best-seller lists. The first ones have been made into movies and are enjoyed by adults as well as children. When a new Harry Potter adventure comes out, some bookstores stay open until midnight so that reserved copies can be picked up on the opening day of their availability.

I find the stories both magical and fascinating and can easily understand their appeal to preteens. For one thing, they're incredibly imaginative. For another, they're classic life stories of an orphan who knows nothing but a miserable life—in Harry's case, with his horrible aunt and uncle and their abominable son, Dudley. When we first meet Harry, his situation is almost hopeless until a mysterious letter arrives by owl messenger. From then on life changes for him. The Potter books are stories of magic, dreams, hope, and survival. And most of all, they appeal to the spirit and enliven it with wonder and awe.

Another book with some of the same strengths is *The Hermit Thrush Sings* by Susan Butler (DK Publishing, 1999). Leora's webbed hand has always marked her as different. She, too, is an orphan and an outcast in her household. She's considered defective and there's always a chance that she'll be sent to the "Institute." After she angers the family sheltering her by freeing a helpless animal, they decide to institutionalize her. How Leora handles the decision and takes her life into her own hands with the help of the baby Birmba is a story of adventure, courage, hidden strengths, and the rewards of caring.

Catechists will be especially interested in heroes and heroines who are also saints. Here are some stories about special saints who have struggled with difference and rejection and have met these and other challenges heroically and compassionately.

Mary Ellen Hynes has written a splendid *Companion to the Calendar: Saints and Mysteries of the Christian Calendar* (Liturgy Training Publications, 1993). It identifies the saint of the day, tells a brief story about each one, and also gives background on the liturgical seasons.

Another interesting and inspiring book about great people is *Explorers for God* by Nathan Aaseng (Augsburg Fortress, 1998). It contains the stories of fifteen men and women whose faith and courage took them into uncharted lands and changed the world forever. This is a good read-aloud book for parents and teachers.

Fear Can Be Calmed by Poetry and Story

In the United States, we've enjoyed freedom and security unparalleled in most countries, even considering what happened to us in New York, Pennsylvania, and the District of Columbia on September 11, 2001. However, in the autumn of 2002 two snipers killed nine and wounded two in the DC metropolitan area where my husband and I were living. Panic and fear were everywhere. For example, when we put gas into our cars, we tried to stay hidden between the car and the gas pump. When we went for a walk, we kept our eyes peeled for a white box truck or van and we strode in crooked, rather than straight, lines. We avidly watched newscasts for the latest information on the possible apprehension of a suspect. Schools kept children inside and most extracurricular activities were canceled. No matter where we went—into stores, restaurants, beauty shops, offices—people were talking about the helplessness all of us felt.

This reality is a different kind of monster from what children fear when it's dark and they're all alone in their rooms. However, this reality makes me more sensitive to what children feel in the wake of their fears. And it has prompted me to reflect on resources that we have to quiet and comfort both ourselves and our children.

Poetry is one of these resources. A special collection is *Emily Dickinson's Letters to the World* by Jeanette Winter (Farrar, Straus and Giroux, 2002). Emily was a recluse. She never went anywhere and her neighbors thought her strange. She always wore white, both in summer and winter. Yet in her reclusiveness and solitude, she wasn't idle. It seems she was constantly writing on sheets and scraps of paper because when she died, her sister Lavinia discovered 1,775 poems that Emily had left behind.

It would enhance and strengthen their spirits were we to give children an opportunity to hear again and again and to learn by heart some of Emily Dickinson's short, beautiful verses. My favorites begin with the lines "I'm Nobody! Who are you?"; "If I can stop one heart from breaking"; "There is no Frigate like a Book"; and "'Hope' is the thing with feathers."

Tales of bravery are another resource. One particularly splendid story is David Wisniewski's *Rain Player* (Clarion Books, 1991). A year of terrible drought threatens a Mayan city, and all the people except Pik, a young ball player, resign themselves to starvation. Pik stakes the city's survival on a game of "pok-atok." It's a powerful original tale of a boy challenging the traditional belief system by taking his fate—and his people's—into his own hands.

Another unique story of facing fear is *Wingwalker* by Rosemary Wells (Hyperion Books for Children, 2002). It's about a frightening period in America when half the people lost every dime they had. The story is told by Reuben, who is just finishing second grade in Ambler, Oklahoma, when a dust storm hits and his parents lose everything. In desperation his father answers an ad, the family moves, and with love and courage they get by.

The kind of terror the United States faced on September 11, 2001, and what we were dealing with a year later in the DC metropolitan area, is all too common in other parts of the world. Families and children are separated and are forced to survive amid bombings, mine fields, and wars without end. *Parvana's Journey* by Deborah Ellis (Publishers Group West, 2002) is an unbelievably painful story of a young girl who leaves Kabul to search for her family (it's also the sequel to *Breadwinner*, mentioned earlier in this chapter). Parvana's father is dead, and her mother, sister, and brother could be anywhere in the country. As she makes her way across the desolate Afghan countryside, she meets other children who are strays from the war. The sad moments described in Parvana's journey provide an honest look at the situation in Afghanistan, yet they never lose sight of the courage and hope that keep children alive even in the most awful circumstances. I consider this book important adult literature for understanding a side of war that is too often hidden.

Stories of Kindness

A long time ago when I was a student at Briar Cliff College in Sioux City, Iowa, I experienced the power of kindness in a teacher. It was a summer session, and two of my courses were logic and metaphysics. Because of the way my mind works, these courses, under normal circumstances, would have been an almost insurmountable challenge. But the circumstances weren't normal because of Sister Bede Klaas. She tailored her teaching to the learning styles of the students, and we all not only mastered the material, we enjoyed it. I actually got an "A" in both courses, which is amazing. Sr. Bede's secret was kindness. She taught carefully, she encouraged, she repeated, she reviewed, and she waited patiently until our minds embraced and owned each piece of the material. She was so gifted at teaching with kindness that she made the most abstract subjects easy and fun.

I thought of Sr. Bede when I read *The Kindness of Children* by Vivian Gussin Paley (Harvard University Press, 1999). It is as much about the kindness of teachers as it is of children. The author is an observer of kindness as it manifests itself in children and is supported by teachers. She also trusts the capacity for kindness in children, and she is gifted in enabling them to tell and act out their kindness stories. Robert Coles, a teacher, author, and psychiatrist, is quoted on the book's jacket. He says, "This is an extraordinarily suggestive book, written for all of us who are interested in children and their educational lives."

Sometimes teachers get so caught up in "teaching" that they lose touch with the heart and spirit of the learners. The pain and hurt blocking productive participation are sometimes intensified by teachers who aren't attuned to what is hidden and unspoken.

A story that addresses this reality is *Speak* by Laurie Halse Anderson (Farrar, Straus and Giroux, 1999). Melinda Sordino, a ninth grader, knows from her first moment at Merryweather High that she's an outcast. She had an end-of-summer party busted by calling the cops—a major infraction in high school society—so her old friends won't talk to her, and people she doesn't know glare at her. Not only are her peers unkind but so are her teachers, who seemingly aren't interested in and are out of touch with "stories" other than the academic ones. The art teacher is the one and only exception.

Melinda retreats into her head and is unable to share the truth of why she had called the cops. However, because of an unfortunate incident, she learns that, although it's hard to speak up for yourself, keeping your mouth shut is worse. This is a story every catechist and teacher should read. It was also a National Book Award Finalist.

Happily, most teachers hear what is unspoken, perceive needs that are hidden, and make a gracious and powerful difference. Children's literature abounds with this kind of story. Here are two:

In *The Art Lesson* by Tomie dePaola (G. P. Putnam's Sons, 1989), Tomie knows from the beginning that he wants to be an artist. He not only wants and needs to be an artist, he convinces his kindergarten teacher and a visiting art teacher to allow him to draw his way, which he continues to do to this day. This is a delightful autobiographical tale.

Thank You, Mr. Falker by Patricia Polacco (Philomel Books, 1998) tells about a child who is unable to read. Her classmates make matters worse by calling her "dummy" and "toad." When she is in fifth grade, a new teacher comes who sees right through the sad little girl to the artist she really is. And when he discovers that she still can't read, he sets out to help her prove to herself that she can. And will! Like Tomie dePaola's story, this one is autobiographical and is Patricia Polacco's personal song of thanks and praise to teachers who quietly but surely change the lives of the children they teach.

Myths, Fables, and Fairy Tales Nurture the Imagination

The love that children, young people, and adults have for the Harry Potter books is not all that surprising because there's a universal interest in myth and magic. However, in reading *Greek Myths: Gods, Heroes, and Monsters* by Ellen Switzer (Atheneum, 1988), I was amazed to learn that of all the original Greek myths, only one has a moral. It's the story of King Midas. Demi, the well-known author and artist, has created her own version of the story, *King Midas and the Golden Touch* (Simon & Schuster Children's Publishing Division, 2002).

King Midas is a proud and foolish king who loves gold above all else. He's granted his wish that everything and every-one he touches will turn to gold. Because of this he can no longer eat and he no longer has any family or friends. The story, accompanied by magnificent illustrations, portrays greed in an unforgettable and magical way. It's an important myth for children because it teaches that when desire gets out of hand, it can cause big trouble.

Another of Demi's creations is a retelling of the Chinese legend *Liang and the Magic Paintbrush* (Henry Holt and Company, 1993). It, too, is about a greedy ruler who misuses a gift given to a young and generous Chinese boy. Still another wonderful story by Demi is *The Empty Pot* (Henry Holt and Company, 1996). This tale is about Ping, the only child in the kingdom who can't grow a flower from the seeds distributed by the emperor. The ending is a complete surprise because of how honesty and integrity are awarded.

Two more of Demi's many unusual and exquisite works are *The Emperor's New Clothes* (Simon & Schuster Children's Publishing Division, 2000) and *Buddha Stories* (Henry Holt and Company, 1997). *The Emperor's New Clothes* is a retelling of Hans Christian Andersen's fairy tale about a proud emperor who does not see what is obvious until he hears the truth from a child. The *Buddha Stories* is a set of parables told by the Buddha to his devoted followers. His message became widespread through fables adapted by famous storytellers like Aesop and LaFontaine. They're important moral tales to pass on to our children who hopefully will pass them to another generation.

Authors often use animals as a way to reach a child's mind and heart. David Macaulay's *Angelo* (Houghton Mifflin Co., 2002) is about an old master plasterer who rescues an injured pigeon while he's restoring the facade of a once-glorious church in Rome. When he can't find a safe place to leave the wounded bird, Angelo becomes the pigeon's reluctant savior. An enduring friendship grows between the pigeon and the old artist. It's a story that captures the imagination and heart in a poignant way.

The Three Questions by John J. Muth (Scholastic Press, 2001) is based on a story by Leo Tolstoy. Young Nikolai is searching for answers to these questions: "When is the best time to do things?" "Who is the most important one?" "What is the right thing to do?"

He seeks counsel from his friends but their answers don't seem quite right. So he seeks out a wise old turtle who helps Nikolai discover the answers in what he does compassionately for others.

Children can never get too much of the magic and mystery that is life. Demi, the author and illustrator, observes that life is magic and that to capture life on paper is magic. Our aim, with children, might be to share as much as we can of life that is captured on paper by exposing them to good literature.

Resources for Building Character

"Character Counts" is a program that is part of character education in Iowa, my home state, as well as in many other states. It has six pillars: trustworthiness, respect, responsibility, fairness, caring, and citizenship. An article on the program (*Des Moines Register*, November 8, 2003) observes that the program fits Iowa perfectly. "In fact," it says, "the six pillars are really just an organized way of teaching Iowa values to kids. This state is about being a good neighbor, working hard, doing what you promise to do, helping those who need help."

Those values fit other states as well. Therefore, character education is increasingly becoming a part of many educational systems. This is prompted, in part, by the instances in our schools and neighborhoods of terrorizing, bullying, hazing, committing suicide, killing, vandalizing, and lesser but still serious acts of disrespect and not caring.

A book that offers strategies to offset what is happening, not only in our schools but also in our homes, is *Coaching Character at Home* by Michael Koehler, PhD (Sorin Books, 2003). It deals with seven principles that the author calls the "7 Cs." They are connectedness, control, commitment, consistency, cooperation, conscience, and competition. It's a splendid and helpful book, written for raising responsible teens, but equally helpful for rearing younger children.

The principles and strategies named above can be reinforced in children and young people by giving them books that are designed for them to use on their own. A striking example is *What Do You Stand For? A Kid's Guide to Building Character* by Barbara Lewis (Free Spirit Publishing, Inc., 1998). The goal of the book, stated in the introduction, is "to help you understand yourself better, to figure out what you stand for—and what you won't stand for."

Besides helping kids gain self-knowledge, self-awareness, self-esteem, and self-actualization (chapter 1), the book also deals with positive attitudes (chapter 2) and specific character traits (chapters 3–26). Each chapter, with the exception of chapter 1, ends with a true story of someone who exemplifies that trait. Teachers and parents, as well as children on their own, might find it an insightful and helpful guide.

Someone whose life exemplifies Michael Koehler's "7 Cs" is runner Wilma Rudolph, whose inspiring story is told in *Wilma Unlimited* by Kathleen Krull (Voyager Books, Harcourt, Inc., 1996).

In Romare Bearden's *Li'l Dan the Drummer Boy: A Civil War Story* (Simon & Schuster Books for Young Readers, 2003), Dan, a child who has been a slave and who loves to play his drum, has nowhere to go after he's set free by Union soldiers. His only recourse is to follow the soldiers, who make him their mascot. When Confederate soldiers attack, Dan realizes that he's the only one who can save his friends and he does it in a heroic way with his drum.

My Brother Martin by Christine King Farris (Simon & Schuster Books for Young Readers, 2003) is a true story about Martin Luther King, Jr., told by his sister. Growing up in Atlanta,

Georgia, he was greatly influenced by his family, especially his father. One event that occurred when he was seven started him on his journey to change the world.

In Eve Bunting's *The Summer of Riley* (Harper Trophy, 2001), after his grandfather's death William and his mother go to the pound and adopt Riley. William falls in love with Riley, and the emptiness of the loss of his grandfather eases. But Riley gets into big trouble and is returned to the pound with the possibility that he'll be put to sleep. What William does to save his dog is a deeply caring story of not giving up, doing everything possible to change the situation, and accepting other painful realities in his life, such as his parents' divorce.

Newbery Award winner *The Bronze Bow* by Elizabeth George Speare (Houghton Mifflin, 1961) is a powerful tale with strong religious overtones. It's about Daniel, a Jewish boy whose father and uncle are killed by Roman centurions. His mother dies shortly after his father's death. Subsequently, he joins a ragtag group in the mountains, who feed his hate of the "conquerors." However, when Jesus, an itinerant preacher, is introduced into his life, he gradually changes. Much of the strength of this tale is its revelation that character is something that is forged over time and through monumental struggles.

6

BOOKS THAT RAISE
MORAL CONSCIOUSNESS

African American Stories and Catechesis

Jeannine Goggin, who died in 2006, was not only a religious educator and great storyteller, but also a dear friend. For years, we gave each other books—ones that we knew the other would enjoy and appreciate. It was an ongoing exchange that kept us mindful of how much our friendship meant.

Some time ago a package arrived from Jeannine with a book by Marybeth Lorbiecki titled *Sister Anne's Hands* (Dial Books for Young Readers, 1998). It's about a religious sister who comes to teach at Anna's school. "Her skin was darker than any person's I'd ever known," says Anna, and her hand "was puppy brown with white lacy moons for nails." Sister Anne was unusual. She brightened up the classroom with her presence and made learning fun. Yet not everyone is happy, and they make this known by sailing a paper plane past Sister Anne's head with a racist message written on it. She deals with the incident in a way that profoundly affects the students and makes this an instructive and timeless tale.

The story surprised me because I thought that what happened to Sister Anne simply wouldn't happen today — that things are different now than when I taught African American children on Chicago's South side in the late fifties. It struck me that racism may be just as operative but more subtle than it was then.

If that is true, religious educators may need to face the issues of racism and prejudice head on, creatively and lovingly, helping children to recognize what it means to be prejudiced, and to own, in a meaningful and practical way, the truth that to be a Catholic Christian is to be open to all people.

Some of this can be done effectively during February — Black History Month. January is a good time to get a jump on preparing special and meaningful ways to celebrate the African American people in our midst.

One of the first things we might do is examine our personal feelings about people of other races, particularly if we belong to a majority group in our area. This is, indeed, a sensitive issue, one that some people might rather not consider, but evidence suggests that we're not wise when we put heads in the sand and decide that all's well racially in our world.

Besides examining our attitudes and feelings, another powerful way to raise consciousness is to read books about blacks on our own and with our children and young people. Here are some excellent suggestions:

In *Amazing Grace* by Mary Hoffman (Dial Books, 1991), schoolmates tell the main character that because she's a girl and black, she can't be Peter Pan in an upcoming play. However, after her mother and grandmother lovingly reaffirm all possibilities, Grace tries out and plays the role to universal acclaim.

Patricia Polacco's *Mrs. Katz and Tush* (Bantam Books, 1992) is a warm and loving story of an African American boy and an elderly Jewish neighbor. *Pink and Say*, also by Polacco

(Philomel Books, 1994), is a multifaceted book that raises questions about courage, war, family, and slavery.

A beautiful picture book biography by Jean Marzollo, *Happy Birthday, Martin Luther King* (Scholastic, 1993), presents Dr. King's life in a simple, direct, and sensitive manner.

In *Jip: His Story* by Katherine Paterson (Lodestar Books, 1996), a young boy falls from a wagon and, unclaimed by anyone, is taken to the town's poor farm. He's a redeeming presence amid the wretched conditions under which the paupers live and, while there, he makes a startling discovery about his origins. Sandra Belton's *Ernestine and Amanda: Mysteries on Monroe Street* (Simon & Schuster, 1998) tells of two African American girls, not quite friends, who are confronted with serious issues involving desegregation and integration.

Escape from Slavery by Doreen Rappaport (HarperCollins, 1991) contains carefully selected escape stories from the lives of fugitive slaves that reveal terrible injustice and amazing courage. In *Yo! Yes?* by Chris Raschka (Orchard Books, 1993), an African American boy and a shy, lonely Caucasian boy discover the possibility of friendship and accept it with enthusiasm.

These are just some of the many available titles about African Americans. Many children's bookstores have displays during Black History Month that might be helpful in adding to the multicultural section of your religious education library.

The Stories of Saints: A Source of Moral and Spiritual Education

Who are our kids' heroes?

Some time ago my niece, Diane Boardman, and her then thirteen-year-old daughter, Allison, spent a week with us. During our time together, the best way to get Allison to participate in our conversations was to ask her questions. When I asked her what she and her friends talk about most, her immediate answer was, "Boys." When I asked her to name someone that she would consider a hero, she named her mother. When I asked her if she had any posters in her room, she said, "Yes," and named 'NSYNC and Britney Spears. Tiger Woods and Lance Armstrong were important, but she didn't consider them heroes, nor did she consider 'NSYNC and Britney Spears heroes or heroine. She's read all the Harry Potter books. He's important, but he wasn't in her hero category either.

Since she attended a Catholic school in Dubuque, Iowa, I asked her if she knew any saints. I really had to push her on this question because she didn't seem to talk about it. But gradually she named, among others, Saints Theresa and Joan of Arc. I wanted to know what she knew about them. She didn't come up with much, but she did say that she knows more about Joan of Arc than any other saint because she had worked on a project about her and seen a movie.

While I was reflecting on the conversation with Allison, I remembered an article that appeared in *The Washington Post Magazine* and in the October 1977 *Reader's Digest*. The article, "What Heroes Teach Us" by Irma Eremia Bragin, concerns what happened to the author's family as a result of her father's acting on his conscience. The inspiration for telling her story came when her son, Andy, as part of his application to a private school had to answer the question, "Who is your hero and why do you admire him?"

Andy knew the story of his grandfather's choice, but his mother didn't know what the story meant to him until the day he burst into her room announcing that he had finished his application essay. Tears ran down her cheeks as she read it:

I got to know a real hero. My Mom's father, Neclo, was put in prison for speaking out against the government. After six years of being shut up alone in a dungeon, he was released. Then my mother, uncle and grandmother left the country. Neclo was not allowed to leave with them.

Learning about Neclo has made standing up for my beliefs very important to me. In fifth grade I wrote my teacher a letter of protest when I felt she had made an unfair decision regarding one of my friends. I am now the student council representative for my class and am fighting hard to make things better at our school. I'm proud of my Romanian grandfather. I hope I get to see him again.

For many young people like Allison and Andy, the people they consider "heroes" are in their families—but we can ensure that they also get to know heroes in their family of faith. Since November starts off with the Feast of All Saints, it's a good time to remember and honor some of these great heroes as well as an ideal time to expose our young people to their stories. As my experience with Allison suggests, getting to know saints may take more than just hearing about them. Working on a project or studying them helps.

Books about saints are being published in increasing numbers. One of them is *Saints: Seventy Stories of Faith* by Alexandra Bonfante-Warren (Courage Books, 2000). The magnificent works of art that are combined with many of the saint stories in this book add a dimension to the lives of these seemingly ordinary people that make them truly extraordinary. This book is a treasure.

Margaret Mulvihill's *The Treasury of Saints and Martyrs* (Penguin Putnam Books for Young Readers, 1999) is remarkable for its full-color pictures, several on each page. The print is unusually attractive and easily readable. The sidebars on many of the pages add interesting information. This and Bonfante-Warren's book above would be a perfect addition to any collection of books on saints.

Finally, *All Saints* by Robert Ellsberg (Crossroad Publishing Co., 1997) is a worthwhile treasury because it does not limit itself to stories of canonized saints but tells about other spiritual giants as well.

Along with introducing children and young people to saints and other great people, it is good to familiarize them with the liturgical seasons in which their lives in the church are rooted. Inos Biffi's *Introduction to the Liturgical Year* (Wm. B. Eerdmans, 1995) is an exquisitely illustrated book to help readers understand the events of the life of Jesus as they are celebrated during the course of the liturgical year. The introduction promises that the book has the possibility of making the life of Jesus attractive to children. It does this by placing the story of Jesus within the memorials and solemnities of the church that mark our liturgical seasons.

Stories That Reflect Diversity Enrich Children's Spirits

After I gave a talk on children's books to a group of Catholic school librarians, one of the librarians expressed appreciation for my suggestion that internationalism be evident in the books that are available to our children. She then told me what had happened during a meeting of principals at their school in which one of the principals was an African American. This principal needed something and asked one of the children to get it for her. The child asked the first adult she met, the librarian, for help. When the librarian asked which of the principals it was, the child became uncomfortable. She didn't seem to want to use the word *black*, wasn't sure how she should describe the woman, and tried to explain by putting her hands up to her face to indicate a difference. The librarian was discomforted by this and quickly saw the potential that stories have to instruct about races and cultures.

The Horn Book printed a lecture by Nina Bawden in which she honored Dorothy Briley, her long-time employee, colleague, and friend. Dorothy was passionately committed to internationalism in children's books as a way of building community among all human beings. Nina remembered her saying that "if anything, homogeneous communities need books that represent the broad spectrum of cultures in the world more than they need books that represent the world that is right outside their front door."

There is great diversity in our communities today. Increasingly, communities are made up of different races, cultures, and ethnic backgrounds. This diversity is well reflected in children's literature. Therefore, it seems wise to use this rich resource as a bridge builder, as a tool to acquaint children with the history in which their classmates and friends are rooted, and as an instructional aid to inform and challenge the racism and prejudice that unfortunately still abounds in our neighborhoods and communities.

Big Jabe by Jerdine Nolan (Lothrop, Lee & Shepard, 2000) is a tall tale with a John Henry–sized hero named Jabe. There's also a Moses-like touch to the story that makes it rich in salvation-history overtones. Jabe is found in a basket in a river by Addy, a young house slave, who scoops him up and sets him on the ground. From that moment Jabe does amazing things to help to save the slaves.

William Miller's *The Piano* (Lee & Low Books, Inc., 2000) is set in the deep south of the early 1900s. A young African

American girl and an older white woman share a love for music through which they forge a friendship that transcends age and race. In the story, a hunger of a young woman's spirit is satisfied, compassion and healing are exercised, and gaps between young and old and between black and white are bridged.

In *The Lotus Seed* by Sherry Garland (Harcourt Brace Jovanovich, 1993) a Vietnamese girl saves a lotus seed and carries it with her when her family is forced to flee bombs and soldiers during a devastating civil war. The importance of the lotus seed, a link to her homeland and her cultural heritage, is poignantly portrayed. She eventually gives seeds from the lotus plant to her children, passing that heritage on to a new generation. The story also provides an insight into what it means to be a refugee and an immigrant.

Mary Ann Hoberman's *And to Think That We Thought That We'd Never Be Friends* (Crown Publishers, Inc., 1999) is an exuberant picture book celebrating friendship, peace, and the removal of barriers to unity. The rhyming text and the jubilant artwork add to the communion that keeps happening in the story.

The more children experience each other's stories, the more they may understand their own place within the human family and their responsibility to be friends.

The Stuff of Dreams Is Found in Stories

When I was an eighth-grader, I graduated from a one-room school in rural Iowa. My dream was to go to high school and become a teacher in that same school. But my father didn't think girls needed a high school education and my mother rarely disagreed with him on important things. So I had to convince him. I promised I'd become a teacher if he would let me go, and I'd also do whatever needed to be done on the farm. This meant getting up early to milk cows by hand and, after school, helping with planting, harvesting, and other chores.

He reluctantly agreed and I kept my promises. After I graduated from high school and got a teaching certificate, I taught in that one-room school. I was only seventeen—in those days, college was not required for teachers—and was too young to receive a paycheck. So it was made out to the director of the school, who happened to be my father.

That long prelude is to interest you in a wonderful novel, *The Secret School* by Avi (Harcourt, Inc., 2001). It's about a girl, like me, who wants to become a teacher. She also has to graduate from eighth grade and go to high school. Wondrously, she manages to do it against even greater odds than I faced. Children who hear or read this story may believe it's pure fiction, unless they learn otherwise. Dreams of an education beyond eighth grade in our country were not always easy to realize, especially for girls, who were expected to become homemakers.

Another story about a dream realized, also against odds, is *I Dreamed I Was a Ballerina* by Anna Pavlova (Metropolitan Museum of Art, 2001). Anna was an only child. Her father died when she was two years old and the family was very poor. Yet, on one of Anna's birthdays, her mother took her to the theater to see the ballet *Sleeping Beauty*. It inspired her to enter the ballet herself. Although she had weak feet and a scrawny body, she turned her limitations into assets and eventually became prima ballerina at the Mariinsky Theater. Thus she fulfilled her dream of dancing in the very place where, as a child, she had seen *Sleeping Beauty*.

A similar story about the realization of a dream is *Alvin Ailey* by Andrea Davis Pinckney (Hyperion Books, 1993). Alvin loves to dance and discovers his own special rhythms. He eventually founds The Alvin Ailey American Dance Theater. His life has left its imprint, as much on the history of the American people as on the history of modern dance.

The workings of a dream are often mysterious. Sometimes when dreams are realized, they don't produce the hoped-for result and the pain can be almost unbearable. This is what happens to Ben, a nine-year-old boy, in Avi's *The Barn* (Avon Books, 1996). His father's grave illness brings Ben home from school and compels him to strive for something great, which is to build the barn that his father talked about before his illness. Ben is sure that it will please his father so much he'll want to live, and he convinces his older sister and brother to help. When the barn is finally built, it doesn't produce the result Ben was certain it would and he's left with some big questions.

Often wishes, like Ben's in the above story, are connected to a desire to help. This is Little Chu's story in *The Master Swordsman*, retold and illustrated by Alice Provensen (Simon & Schuster, 2001). Little Chu's village is repeatedly ravaged by bandits. He wants to learn how to protect it and he goes in search of a master swordsman who could teach him a way to save his people. But when he finds the master swordsman, he tells Little Chu that he no longer teaches as he is old and needs help. Little Chu generously agrees to help and works hard. Gradually the master swordsman seems to treat Little Chu badly but, in doing so, he teaches him what he needs to know and provides him with a gift that greatly helps his family and the people in his village.

Children have dreams. Reading or telling them this kind of story can help them believe in their dreams and appreciate that what happens doesn't always look like what was hoped for, yet is a dream realized.

Saintliness and Story

As I was thinking about November and saints, it occurred to me that the question "What makes someone a saint?" is a good one to ask. I've found that many children find their answer close to home—namely, in their parents. One of the most touching answers I've received is a sixth-grader's. He wrote: "My Mom can't stop herself from giving stuff away to the poor. Good stuff! I have to hide clothes I want to keep because I know that if I don't she'll give them away. She makes us mad sometimes by her 'givingawayness' but when it comes down to what makes a hero, she really is mine." As a postscript, he added, "We really do have way more than we need and she knows it, but she also gives away things that we need. Her answer is always, They need it more than we do!"

This boy described saintliness in terms of his mother's giving to others, not only out of their abundance, but also to a point of sacrifice. He also suggests that her holiness is directly related to her way of being in the world, which he names her "givingawayness."

This same kind of goodness is reflected in *The Dancing Man* by Ruth Lecher Bornstein (Houghton Mifflin, 1998), a story about an orphan boy named Joseph who lives in a poor village by the Baltic Sea. While he is young, Joseph realizes that life in the village is dreary and hard. No one laughs, no one dances. But he sees that all around him the world dances. He dreams that one day he will dance down the road from village to village, even as far as the southernmost sea. But he tells no one because he knows no one will understand.

Then one evening a mysterious stranger appears on the shore, sweeps off his hat, bows, and says to Joseph, "I'm the

Dancing Man and I have a gift for you." The old man dances down the shore and Joseph follows. A sharp gust of wind blows Joseph around and when he turns back, the man is gone but in the sand lie his silver shoes. Joseph knows they are meant for him.

Joseph grows up and one day the shoes fit. He puts them on and dances from village to village, taking away some of the dreariness and bringing happiness to the people. The story ends as it begins, with Joseph passing on to another child what had been given to him.

This is essentially what we do when we hand on to children stories of people who have lived in a way that is holy, selfless, noble, admirable, or virtuous. Most children, like Joseph, dream of making a difference and they experience a longing to fulfill those dreams. They admire and are inspired by goodness and greatness.

November is a good month to introduce them to saintly people. Here are a few of the many books for doing this:

- *Early Saints of God* by Bob Hartman (Augsburg, 1998)

- *Young Mary of Nazareth* by Marianna Mayer (Morrow Junior Books, 1998)

- *Who's Who in the Bible* by Dr. Stephen Motyer (D. K. Publishing, 1998)

- *Joan of Arc* by Josephine Poole (Alfred A. Knopf, 1998)

7

BIBLE STORYBOOKS AND STORIES OF TRANSFORMATION

Bible Storybooks for Children

Parents, catechists, religion teachers, and others buying baptism, first communion, and confirmation gifts have frequently asked me to suggest a Bible for using or giving to children and young people. Over the years I've collected a sizable number of Bibles for children, and today it's getting increasingly difficult to keep up with the many that are on the market. I'm not sure why the interest in retelling Bible stories has grown, but it has. This development creates a real challenge in determining which ones are good, better, and best.

I will not critique from a scholarly vantage point here, but will simply reflect on a Bible's merit from my enjoyment and use of it with children and young people. Among the things that I look for are the beauty and depth of the visuals, the artistry of the telling while adhering to the original story, the movement and rhythm of the words and phrases, the feeling for the story that comes through the characters in it, and the way the words that are used inspire and create mind-pictures of what is happening.

My favorite—the one that does all of these things well—is *The Doubleday Illustrated Children's Bible* by Sandol Stoddard, with paintings by Tony Chen (Doubleday, 1983). This I consider an excellent children's Bible for teacher use and for bedtime reading. The stories are more developed than in some others. The paintings are unusually beautiful and perceptively portray the inner workings and truth of a story. While using this Bible, I've sometimes had to pull the children away from the pictures because they get caught in the activity and mystery in them. Most of the paintings are indeed spellbinding. The paintings of Daniel surrounded by crouching and somewhat puzzled lions and of Jesus and his disciples around the Last Supper table are my favorites. Another thing about the paintings that utterly fascinates me is the portrayal and movement of people's hands.

For very young children, Sandol Stoddard and Tony Chen have abbreviated the stories and enlarged the paintings in *A Child's First Bible Storybook* (Inspirational Press, 1998).

Another that I rate highly for young readers is *The Children's Illustrated Bible* with stories retold by Selina Hastings and illustrated by Eric Thomas (Dorling Kindersley, 1994). This Bible appeals to me because of the information that is added, both visually and verbally, to explain the stories and to set them in their historical and geographical context. There are sidebars on every page that include maps and photographs of people, plants, animals, and artifacts related to the stories. I have found, however, that some of the children with whom I've used this Bible are less interested in the sidebars than I am.

Dorling Kindersley has published other Bible storybooks that are of high quality and similar in the way the stories are presented visually and verbally. Among them are *A First Bible Storybook* with stories retold by Mary Hoffman and illustrated by Julie Downing (DK Publishing, Inc., 1977), and *The DK Illustrated Family Bible*, edited by Dr. Claude-Bernard Costecalde and illustrated by Peter Dennis (1997).

A Bible that I like enough to enthrone in my office and give as a baptismal gift is *The Beginner's Bible*, told by Karyn Henley and illustrated by Dennas Davis (Questar Publishers, Inc., 1989).

Using the Contemporary English Version, Children of Color Publishing has thoughtfully and prayerfully designed the *Children of Color Storybook Bible* with illustrations by Victor Hogan (Thomas Nelson, 1997). This I consider a special and welcome addition to any collection of children's Bibles because it is created especially for young people of African descent. The note to parents at the front of the book explains the intent of those preparing it as well as the value of God's word in the lives of children.

More Bible Storybooks for Children

Earlier, I identified criteria that I use for assessing Bible books for children and I recommended specific ones. This chapter will briefly describe some others and then offer a bibliography.

One of the most complete Bible storybooks for children is *The Bible: A People Listen to God* by Joan Baro i Cerqueda with illustrations by Maria Ruis (The Liturgical Press, 1998). Each story is carefully and clearly told and each illustration fits perfectly, adding the kind of grace and beauty that stirs the imagination and holds the eye. This Bible is truly a treasure and I recommend it highly.

Someone who is truly gifted at retelling and illustrating Bible stories is Tomie dePaola. This is evident in *Tomie dePaola's Book of Bible Stories* (G. P. Putnam's Sons, 1990). He is faithful to biblical texts, making occasional slight changes only in order to make them comprehensible to children. His retelling of "Esther Saves Her People" is a good example. I've found that children pick up dePaola's love for the people in the stories and his reverence for the sacred events. And best of all, there is not the slightest hint of moralizing about peoples' response to God's action.

DePaola also does a superb job with the parables. The best book of these, from my perspective and experience, is his *The Parables of Jesus* (Holiday House, 1987), which includes twenty-seven parables based closely on the biblical texts. The illustrations, in dePaola's inimitable style, are not only delightful, they also reveal each parable's message while at the same time capturing its mystery. This is one that I like to give as a first communion gift.

Tell Me the Bible by Joelle Chabert, Francois Mourvillier, and Letizia Galli (The Liturgical Press, 1991) is one of the better of the children's Bibles that are as much picture books as storybooks. The constant interplay of word and picture makes it easy for children to remember the people and events in the stories. Children who can't yet read, after hearing and seeing the stories, can often retell them. And I have been surprised by some children who pick up the spirit and the mystery in the stories—that which is not apparent in either the words or the pictures on the pages.

Another of the Bibles with a good interplay of word and picture is *The Kingfisher Children's Bible*, retold by Ann Pilling and illustrated by Kady MacDonald Denton (Kingfisher Books, 1993).

The best one of the word-and-picture type is of a single Bible story—*Noah's Ark* by Peter Spier (Doubleday, 1997), which won the Caldecott Medal (the chief award for picture books, although it is given for the illustrations). The drawings are incredibly detailed, often humorous, and sometimes moving. This is a near-perfect retelling and picturing of one of the most often-told Bible stories for children.

Some of the most successful retellings of single Bible stories for children are the Arch Books by Concordia Publishing House. Their success stems in great part from the fact that the texts are in rhyming verse. Among the many Arch Books that I like, my all-time favorites are *Amrah and the Living Water* by Anne Jennings (1976), *Eight Bags of Gold* (1964) and *The Rich Fool* (1964), both by Janice Kramer, and Dave Hill's *The Boy Who Gave His Lunch Away* (1967).

A most unusual retelling of Bible stories for children is *Let My People Go* by Patricia McKissack, illustrated by James E. Ransome (Simon & Schuster, 1998). Price Jeffries, a fictionalized free black abolitionist, uses his distinctive voice to tell his daughter, Charlotte, twelve stories from the Old Testament, in response to questions that she asks him in the context of an incident in her young life.

Other children's Bibles that are worth considering for catechetical or family use include these:

- *Bible Stories for Children* by Geoffrey Horn and Arthur Cavanaugh (Simon & Schuster, 1980)

- *A Family Treasury of Bible Stories* by Roberto Brunelli (Harry N. Abrams, Inc., 1997)

- *The Illustrated Jewish Bible for Children* by Selina Hastings (DK Publishing, Inc., 1997)

- *The Rhyme Bible* by L. J. Sattgast (Questar Publishers, 1996)

- *The Lion Storyteller Bible* by Bob Hartman (Lion Publishing, 1995)

- *My First Picture Bible* by Eira Reeves (Moody Press, 1998)

Stories of Transformation

Story has the power to transform lives—our own and those of our students and children. It is good, therefore, both to read and to read about stories.

To read about story, I recommend once again Maureen Gallagher's *The Art of Catechesis* (Paulist Press, 1998), particularly chapter 4, "Story and Imagination." Maureen makes a convincing case for the teaching value of stories and also describes how they clarify the truth, offer opportunities to laugh and cry, awaken spiritual awareness, heal wounds, build memory banks, and unite communities. She believes that without story, "Propositions about faith are dull and lifeless," and that "stories are the tool of the catechist as a brush is the tool of a painter."

Another "must read" is *Gospel Light* by John Shea (Crossroad Publishing Co., 1998). John is an inveterate believer in the power of story and has spent his life looking at humanity, mystery, and grace through that perspective. In this book, he takes the Jesus stories and helps us to understand them as tools of spiritual transformation step-by-step. This is the best book on Gospel stories that I have ever read.

Since spiritual transformation is a primary goal of religion teachers and catechists, stories, from both the Gospels and sacred and secular literature, are key resources.

Be Not Far from Me: Legends from the Bible as retold by Eric Kimmel (Simon & Schuster, 1998) reveals the tumultuous relationship between people and God that started four thousand years ago and continues to this day. It begins with the story of Abraham and ends with the story of Daniel. The author draws from both the Bible and midrash to create vivid portrayals of twenty biblical heroes. The characters come to life through a developed and colorful telling that adds immeasurably to our ability to understand them and their place in salvation history. This book is a great resource for adding to children's and young people's knowledge and appreciation of their ancestors, the people of the Hebrew Scriptures. I came away from the stories with a feeling of awe for and familiarity with the biblical heroes and with a deepened sense of God's presence and activity in our lives and in the world. It's an amazing book.

Douglas Kaine McKelvey's *The Angel Knew Papa and the Dog* (Penguin Putnam Books, 1998) is truly what Cynthia Rylant, herself a superb children's author, claims: "A small masterpiece." A little girl describes her life with her father. Her mother died the year she was born, so for her it has always been the two of them. Loneliness is kept at bay with days that are filled with chores and nights that are filled with papa's singing and candle-light reading. All is well until the rains come and don't stop. Papa is swept away and the little girl has to face the flood alone. She thinks everything is lost, until help comes from an unexpected source.

This is a story of a little girl, but also of a loving father. Children who read or hear this story may have a sense of what is meant when they hear God described as a loving father. That angels are a part of life is also something that the story reveals, and, last but not least, it also suggests what story can mean in a child's life and how it transforms reality.

The Muffin Child by Stephen Menick (Penguin Putnam Books, 1998) is set in a small Balkan farming village. Eleven-year-old Tanya faces life alone after her parents are swept away by a flooding river. Denying her loss, she continues to perform daily chores and makes muffins each day in preparation for her parents' return. Life is hard for Tanya, and the community that surrounds her is somehow unable to be helpful in a redeeming way. In the story, basic human traits of greed, love, and self-preservation are examined, and a family story is passed on to a new generation.

Encouraging children and young people to read and to listen to the kind of stories mentioned above can enhance and transform their spirits.

8

POETRY

Poetry Can Be a Direct Transfusion of Hope, Calm, or Compassion

Former poet laureate Rita Dove, writing about country doctor and poet William Carlos Williams, observed that Williams "knew that health is not merely a matter of passing a physical exam. We can think ourselves in top shape and still suffer from malnutrition of the spirit. Poetry, that briefest yet most intense of communications, can be a direct transfusion of hope or calm or compassion—a sort of I.V. for the soul" ("Book World," *The Washington Post*, January 20, 2000).

I love to read poetry to and with children and do so frequently. Invariably, a stillness settles over them, sometimes laughter bubbles up and spills over, and sometimes their faces screw up in an attempt to comprehend what the poet is saying. I rarely read a poem once—most often two or three times. Rarely do I ask a child to read a poem aloud to the class unless he or she has mastered the phrasing and rhythm and has a feeling for the inner world of the poem.

One of my best memories of enjoying poetry with children happened in Dubuque, Iowa. In art class, the children and I made small wooden boats with scraps for sails. Then we took them to the nearby Mississippi River, read Emily Dickinson's "'Twas such a little, little boat," put our boats out to sail, and watched with delight and sadness as they disappeared. What the last line of her poem says—"My little craft was lost!"—was true of each one of ours.

I invite you, if you're not already there, into books of poetry and encourage you to taste and savor. Here are some that I especially like and recommend.

The poems in Ann Whitford Paul's *All by Herself* (Browndeer Press/Harcourt Brace & Co., 1999) recount the stories of fourteen girls who performed acts of daring determination and heroic courage at a young age. Some of them became famous, like Amelia Earhart, Mary Jane McLeod, Rachel Carson, Wilma Rudolph, Wanda Gag, Pocahontas, and Golda Mabovitch (Golda Meir). The poems are fast-paced and capture the spirit as well as the mettle of each woman. They provide a tempting taste of history.

The subtitle of *Pierced by a Ray of Sun*, selected by Ruth Gordon (HarperCollins Children's Books, 1995), is *Poems About the Times We Feel Alone*. The small blurb on the book jacket says that the poems are "about all of us, for we all sometimes feel we are different and alone." There are seventy-three poems in this collection and some of them make me cry. Perhaps I'm more prone to tears because while writing this I learned about a fifteen-year-old's suicide. I wish someone had read to him Joseph Hutchinson's "The One Armed Boy," "A Half Blade of Grass" by Yevgeny Yevtushenko, or "Birth Elegy VI" by Natalie Robins. It might have helped.

A beautiful book that combines art and poetry is Jan Greenberg's *Heart to Heart: New Poems Inspired By Twentieth-Century American Art* (Harry N. Abrams, Inc., 2001.). Each image inspired the poem that accompanies it and represents the most important artistic movements of the past century.

Poetry Has the Power to Transport Children

When our minds and hearts are filled with poetry, we're provided with what Marcel Proust calls "involuntary memory" — that which is spontaneously given back to us, as if by magic, unconsciously.

I was not immersed in poetry as a child, but I've immersed many children in it. I believe that this is probably the best thing that I've done with them. Because of my experience of reading poetry to and with children, I've developed an insatiable love and hunger for its beauty and power, and a passion for developing that in others.

I'm not surprised that there's been a greater turning to poetry since September 11, 2001. A book that's a perfect example of this is *Facing Fear with Faith* by Arthur Jones and Dolores Leckey (Thomas More, 2002). In the introduction to the book Leckey says, "To change ourselves to face fear requires a journeying into deeper, easier—even happier, or at least more comfortably resigned and trusting—reliance on God." Then she adds: "The starting point, as it must be, is with poetry."

The authors weave sixty poems into the text to help the reader use what they call tools like faith, hope, love, prayer, and contemplation to face fear.

I hope that poetry will become an everyday part of your teaching so that whole poems or bits and pieces of them become a part of your students' involuntary memories. Building poetry into your classes is as easy as finding poems you enjoy. Choose selections, try them out on your students, and when you find some that they like as well, read them over and over. One year, while I was teaching a class of fourth- and fifth-graders at Corpus Christi on Chicago's South Side, a poem that the children begged me to read over and over again was "Casey at the Bat" by Ernest Lawrence Thayer. I read many poems to them but "Casey at the Bat" was their favorite for reasons too mysterious to define. It is also one of my favorites, because often in life I've metaphorically gotten up to bat at a critical moment and struck out.

Here are some really fine collections of poetry for children:

The Oxford Illustrated Book of American Poems, edited by Donald Hall (Oxford University Press, 1999), includes some of the best of American children's poetry—poems that every child should hear, poems that may have been neglected or forgotten; for example, "The Village Blacksmith," "The Blind Men and the Elephant," "Little Orphan Annie," "Casey at the Bat," and "I'm Nobody! Who are You?"

The poems in *Lives: Poems about Famous Americans*, selected by Lee Bennett Hopkins (Harper Collins, 1999), are about sixteen important American personalities who changed the course of history, leaving an indelible mark on the entire world. They include Abraham Lincoln, Thomas Alva Edison, Eleanor Roosevelt, Rosa Lee Parks, and Sacagawea.

In *My America: A Poetry Atlas of the United States*, also selected by Lee Bennett Hopkins (Simon & Schuster, 2000), fifty poems—grouped by geographic region—create a remarkable portrait of America in all its stunning variety. No matter where you and your children live, a poem describes something that is remarkable, moving, and splendid about it. Besides the poems, the book contains maps of the regions, fascinating facts for each state, and delightful artwork.

In the introduction to *The Random House Book of Poetry for Children*, selected by Jack Prelutsky (Random House, 1983),

Prelutsky tells of working directly with children. He did this because he had found that many children "at some point during their school careers seem to lose their interest and enthusiasm for poetry. They begin to find it boring and irrelevant, too difficult, or too dull to bother with." In reading and reciting poetry with children, he began "to understand the kinds of poems to which children respond—poems that cause a palpable ripple of surprise by the unexpected comparisons they make, poems that paint pictures with words that are as vivid as brushstrokes, poems that reawaken pleasure in the sounds and meaning of language." This comprehensive anthology is the result of his findings and may be the best book with which to begin.

Stories and Poetry Are Tools to Reveal Heroism and Holiness

Since 9/11, heroes have been on our minds. We more quickly take note of unselfish and extraordinary actions, whereas previously we may have taken them for granted. It's not that we haven't recognized and honored heroism in the past—but today we seem to value it with an intensity that I find inspiring and energizing. I also find that these acts by heroic people give me new reasons for hope.

We will never forget what police officers and firefighters did in the aftermath of 9/11. I hope that we'll also long remember the hundred professionals who worked feverishly during three days in July 2002 to drill nine Pennsylvania miners to an escape shaft, and that we won't forget Erica Pratt, the seven-year-old hostage who with uncommon determination and perseverance escaped from her captors. Eric Cooper, president of the National Urban Alliance for Effective Education in Stamford, Connecticut, observed, "What we need are more children like Erica who exhibit advanced thinking skills, such as the ability to solve problems and make the appropriate decisions. Erica teaches all of us to persevere rather than surrender to the challenges life often presents" (*USA Today*, July 9, 2002).

Perhaps we need to accept that most, if not all, students will respond to continually higher levels of expectation. But unless we narrow the gaps between rich and poor and black and white, we condemn many to underachievement.

One of the things we're challenged to do is enable heroism and success. We can do this, in part, by showing children what those qualities look like and by doing everything in our power to help them achieve some of both.

One way to do that is to read them stories of heroic men, women, and children. Rebecca Hazell has written three: *Heroines: Great Women Through the Ages* (Abbeville Press Publishers, 1996); *Heroes: Great Men Through the Ages* (Abbeville Press Publishers, 1997); and *The Barefoot Book of Heroic Children* (Barefoot Books, 2000). In her introduction to *Heroines* the author says, "When we think of heroism, we may imagine dramatic rescues and daring deeds, or picture someone risking his or her life to save someone wounded or in danger. These kinds of heroism don't happen every day.

"Other kinds of heroism last for a lifetime. Some people lead heroic lives by being brave or kind, and others are heroic because of their ability to see or do things in a new way."

In the introduction to *Heroic Children* she writes, "Even when you're young, your voice can count; your example can change other people's attitudes; your opinion does matter. It may seem to you that all the people you are expected to look up to and admire are adults, but they were once young as well. In many cases, the seeds of their greatness lay in what they did during their childhood."

Among the people featured in Rebecca Hazell's books are Joan of Arc, Sacagawea, Harriet Tubman, Amelia Earhart, Socrates, Leonardo da Vinci, Mohandas Gandhi, Albert Einstein, Martin Luther King, Jr., Anne Frank, Pocahontas, Helen Keller, and Sadako Sasaki.

We the People by Bobbi Katz (Greenwillow Books, 2000) is a most wonderful collection of sixty-five original poems that depict people and events throughout the history of the United States.

Two unusual books about saints, written by Michael O'Neill McGrath and published by Liturgy Training Publications, are *Patrons and Protectors: Occupations* (2001) and *Patrons and Protectors: More Occupations* (2002). The author delightfully describes saints as patrons of particular occupations. For example, St. Ann is the patron of homemakers; Francis de Sales patron of journalists and writers; Therese of Lisieux patron saint of airplane pilots; and John the Baptist patron saint of road workers.

All of these books can introduce children and young people to heroism and holiness and, perhaps, enable them to discover in themselves seeds of both.

9

NURTURING THE SPIRIT

A Tribute to Sister Wendy Beckett

The British nun Sister Wendy Beckett has retired from her television career. She's in her 70s and in declining health, and is finding it increasingly difficult to travel. She plans to spend most of her retirement in contemplation.

Megan Rosenfeld, a staff writer for *The Washington Post*, claims that Sister Wendy has done almost as much for art as Julia Child has done for food. "Her perspective is endearingly Catholic in the original meaning of the word," says Rosenfeld, "as respectful of non-Christian religions as of her own deeply held beliefs. To her, art is a spiritual experience and creativity a holy process."

I've followed Sister Wendy's career and have collected most of her amazing and stunningly beautiful books about art. I'm fascinated by her sense that there's a story behind every work. Because of Sister Wendy, art has become for me a primary resource for teaching religion and an inspiring resource for personal meditation and prayer. My gratitude to her is boundless. I believe that as catechists, the more we use art, the more we widen the eyes of our learners to mystery, the more we engage their spirits in reflecting on life and the presence of God in the whole of it.

Here are my favorites of Sister Wendy's many books:

In *Sister Wendy's Book of Meditations* (DK Publishing, Inc., 1998), the author uses art to illustrate each meditation and shares her unique personal insights into the blessings and inner calm of silence, peace, love, and joy.

Thirty-five saints are celebrated in *Sister Wendy's Book of Saints* (Dorling Kindersley, 1998). The way Sister Wendy sees each saint is both fascinating and inspiring. This is a near-perfect book for introducing children and young people to heroic and holy people in their Catholic Christian tradition. A calendar of feast days, at the end of the book, is an added plus.

In *Sister Wendy: My Favorite Things* (Henry N. Abrams, 1999), she talks intimately and sensitively about seventy-five works of art from around the world. Her words echo what I deeply believe: "It is hard to explain what makes a work of art beautiful. I think the best way is to say that you never get tired of looking at it, that you always see more in it, that it gives you a sense of being satisfied, of being at peace yet alive and eager." This collection contains Carlo Crivelli's multifaceted and incredibly interesting *The Annunciation, with Saint Emidius.* It might take a whole religion class to enter fully into the story of the Annunciation depicted in this painting.

Perhaps her greatest published work is *Sister Wendy's 1,000 Masterpieces* (DK Publishing, Inc., 1999). In the foreword she states, "This is a book where the pictures alone matter; the purpose of the text is to keep you in the presence of the painting. Look long enough, and each one will work its magic on you."

Sister Wendy also produced a book specifically for children — *A Child's Book of Prayer in Art* (Dorling Kindersley, Inc., 1995). Her note to parents and teachers at the beginning of the book says, "This book is really self-contained and in many cases the best thing for an adult to do is simply stay clear—let children get on with the book alone. But for some children (especially younger children), there is definitely a place for adult involvement."

A Tribute to Fred Rogers

Fred McFeely Rogers, 74, died of stomach cancer on February 27, 2003. On the following day the *Dubuque Telegraph Herald* carried the headline, "Sad day in the neighborhood: Mister Rogers dies." Beneath the headline was this tribute: "Star of children's show is remembered as a man who always had time to talk to young people."

Having been privileged to know Fred Rogers personally and being very familiar with his show, I mourned his death. This was a man who never wavered in the mission he considered his min- istry: to use his "Neighborhood" to persuade young viewers to love themselves and others. As Robert Bianco observed, "Television has produced many stars. It has nurtured fewer great men. Rogers was both" (*USA Today*, February 28, 2003).

Through music and a deep understanding of child devel- opment, Rogers helped young viewers deal with grown-up issues such as death, war, prejudice, and disabilities. His main message to children never changed: "You are lovable just as you are." But he also asked them to be better than they might be—to be kind, to be open, to be imaginative. He taught them how to share, how to deal with anger, and how to be tolerant. And he soothed them with rituals.

Another significant part of Rogers' legacy is that he taught parents how to talk to their children about difficult issues. Underlying his incredibly effective ministry of dealing with the emotional life of children was his belief that "at the center of the universe is a loving heart that continues to beat and that wants the best for every person. Anything we can do to foster the intellect and spirit and emotional growth of our fellow human beings, that is our job. Those of us who have this particular vision must continue against all odds. Life is for service."

Books are a great resource for continuing Mister Rogers' ministry. Here are some that do that well:

By Fred Rogers:

You Are Special: Words of Wisdom for All Ages from a Beloved Neighbor (Viking Press, 1994); *Mister Rogers Talks with Parents,* with Barry Head (Hal Leonard Publishing, 1993); *Dear Mister Rogers, Does It Ever Rain in Your Neighborhood?* (Penguin, 1996); *The Giving Box: Create a Tradition of Giving with Your Children* (Running Press, 2000).

And by other authors, in his spirit:

In *I'm Gonna Like Me,* by Jamie Lee Curtis with illustrations by Laura Cornell (HarperCollins, 2002), through alternating a girl's and a boy's points of view the text and the artwork show kids that the key to feeling good is liking yourself because you are you.

I Love You This Much by Lynn Hodges and Sue Buchanan and illustrated by John Bendall Brunello (Zondervan, 2001) is a moving story about love between a parent and child, based on a beautiful lullaby, *I Love You this Much.* A CD of the lullaby is included with the book.

Guess How Much I Love You, by Sam McBratney and illustrated by Anita Jeram (Candlewick Press, 1995), is a delightful and memorable tale of affection. Every time little Nutbrown Hare demonstrates how much he loves his father, Big Nutbrown Hare gently shows him that the love is returned even more.

In the novel *Maggie's Door* by Patricia Reilly Giff (Wendy Lamb Books, 2003), Sean and Nory have a dream of reaching

America and the door of their sister's and brother's home. They are propelled on a most difficult and harrowing journey by love as well as by the memories of people who taught them to keep going, no matter what, and to believe in the possible, in spite of terrible odds. It's a classic example of the use of imagination, openness, and kindness that Mister Rogers encouraged in children.

Pictures of Hollis Woods by Patricia Reilly Giff (Random House, 2002) is the story of Hollis, a young artist who has been in so many foster homes she can't remember them all. An elderly art teacher who is quirky and affectionate, and a family who want her and offer her a home, make all the difference.

To feed children's imaginations with these kinds of stories is to strengthen their spirits and inspire them to share their own ideas and experiences of what love and courage look like.

Good Literature Enlightens and Enhances Our Hearts and Minds

A splendid piece of literature, whether for children or adults, inserts itself into our inner consciousness in such a way that our memory feeds on it and our spirit is enlivened. This is what *The Secret Life of Bees* by Sue Monk Kidd (Penguin Books, 2002) does. Although I rarely refer to adult fiction, this book is so special I'm making an exception.

The book is about twelve-year-old Lily Owens, whose life has been shaped around the blurred memory of the afternoon her mother was killed. In getting to know Lily, we become deeply immersed in how children process the realities that engulf them. We are further awakened to their self-talk as they search for meaning and cope with decisions and their consequences. This story also brings us into painful touch with racism as it was practiced in the South and how love and acceptance in a child's life make the needed difference.

Most of us have a sense that some of the children we work with are in pain, coping with situations that we can't even imagine. For example, a child in one of my sixth-grade religion classes responded to the statement "Name one thing that makes you afraid" by writing, "I'm afraid of everyone in my family except my sister."

Literature reveals the self-talk of children and young people as they deal with their relationships with adults and with each other. Literature shows the ways in which prejudice and different cultures affect young people's identities, and what it means to care in such a way that it makes a difference in the lives of others.

Here is a small sampling of these stories:

Gracie's Girl by Ellen Wittlinger (Aladdin Paperbacks, 2000) tells the story of Bess Cunningham, a middle schooler, who is part of a family that cares about the poor. A reluctant helper at the homeless shelter where her Mom and Dad volunteer, Bess gradually grows in appreciation of the difficulties faced by the homeless, especially that of an elderly woman named Gracie. She also grows in her realization that there are different ways of becoming popular and valued.

The setting for Linda Sue Park's *The Kite Fighters* (Dell Yearling, 2000) is Seoul, Korea. It's about a kite-flying competition that happens once a year. Two brothers struggle with a tradition in which the older brother is expected to represent the family— however, the younger brother is more gifted at kite flying. How they deal with both their tradition and their different gifts allows for the older brother to carry on his responsibility for his family's honor and for the younger brother to achieve his own greatness.

Grover G. Graham and Me by Mary Quattlebaum (Dell Yearling, 2001) is the story of Ben Watson. Headed for his eighth foster home, Ben is a child of the system that he thinks he has figured out. The main rule is not to get attached. But then a baby at his new home, also a foster child, captures his heart. Also, his new foster parents, the Torgies, understand and care for him in a way that helps him to trust and to grow, in that he's able to make a big mistake and still remain with them. This story simply and gently gives a glimpse of what it is like for some children caught in the foster-care system.

The picture book *It's Okay to Be Different* by Todd Parr (Little, Brown & Company, 2001) teaches that all creatures are unique and okay just the way they are, a fact often not sufficiently appreciated by either oneself or by others. This is a good choice to nurture acceptance of differences and to cultivate nonprejudicial attitudes.

Max Lucado's *Small Gifts in God's Hands* (Tommy Nelson, 2000) imaginatively and simply retells one of the most compassionate and caring stories in the New Testament ("The Boy Whose Lunch Fed Thousands," Matt 14:19–21; Mark 6:39–44; Luke 9:14–17; John 6:10–14). It would be good to read this with your children before or after they hear this Gospel proclaimed during a Sunday Mass.

None of these books compares with the Harry Potter tales, so expecting children to get overly excited about them is perhaps expecting too much. Their main value may be in what happens to adults who read them. Helping adults get in touch with the vulnerabilities of our children and young people is one of the best things that children's literature does.

Picture Books Nurture Children's Spirits

In his acceptance speech for the Caldecott Award for *My Friend Rabbit*, Eric Rohman explained why picture books are vital in children's lives. Children are visually aware, he said, more so than most adults, because that's what they do. He contends that a child's primary job from birth to eight years is to observe the world, to learn how things work. Children, he observed, are hard-wired to be curious.

By using picture books in our religion classes, we can tap into children's imaginations, visual awareness, and curiosity. Following are some that are both delightful and instructive:

In *Sylvester and the Magic Pebble* by William Steig (Aladdin Paperbacks, 1969; Caldecott Medal, 1970), Sylvester finds a magic pebble and, in a moment of fright, he asks his pebble to turn him into a rock. But then he can't hold the pebble to wish himself back to normal. How he finally becomes himself again is a wonderful book of hope being realized.

Aaron Shepard's *The Princess Mouse: A Tale of Finland* (Atheneum Books, 2003) is about two sons and their search for a bride. The oldest son knows the woman he wants to marry and carries out his father's instructions accordingly. The younger son also follows his father's instructions, but it leads to the most unusual of sweethearts. What happens proves that with an open heart and mind, love can be rewarded in the most surprising and unexpected ways.

In Douglas Wood's fable *The Old Turtle* (1991; Scholastic Press edition, 2001) a wise old turtle, with quiet eloquence, reminds all creatures of their connection to God, to the earth, and to one another. This book received the Abby Book of the Year Award in 1993 from the American Booksellers and International Reading Associations. In Wood's *Old Turtle and the Broken Truth* (Scholastic Press, 2003), people discover a powerful truth that gives them strength and happiness, but they don't see that their truth is broken and incomplete. And because they do not share their truth with other people and other beings, all the earth begins to suffer. Then a little girl sets out to find the ancient wise one known as Old Turtle. He helps her to hear again the language of breezes...and passes on the precious piece of wisdom that will mend the people's broken truth.

Dog Heaven by Cynthia Rylant (The Blue Sky Press, 1995) is a gentle and insightful story of what dog heaven is like: a place of mystery, a place that follows death, a place that both adults and children wonder about.

In *Thank You Grandpa* by Lynn Plourde (Dutton Children's Books, 2003), as grandfather and granddaughter enjoy many walks through the woods, they make many discoveries—a bee sipping nectar, a sneaky snake, teardrops of dew on a spiderweb. One day after finding a dead grasshopper, the child wonders what they might do. Her grandfather suggests saying "Thank you and goodbye," which they do with a simple burial ceremony. This begins a ritual of "praying tribute" to other creatures on their nature walks. Finally the day arrives when the granddaughter walks alone but her grandfather's lessons remain. And she says, "Thank you, Grandpa, for sharing spiderweb tears and firefly flashes. But most of all, thank you for teaching me the words I need to say, 'Thank you and goodbye.'"

The Jade Necklace by Paul Yee (Crocodile Books, 2002) tells the story of Yen Yee and her family in South China. One night her fisherman father vanishes in a ferocious storm at sea. But it is not only her father that she suddenly loses—her mother accepts an offer to send Yen Yee to the New World with a family to care for their daughter. Yen Yee also feels betrayed by the ocean, a friend she has trusted all her life. However, when it gives her back something precious and there's a chance that she'll be reunited with her mother and brother, the story becomes one of love and forgiveness, of bravery and community.

This is only a small sampling of good picture books. Leo Lionni, a master storyteller and picture book author, also has many titles that can be used catechetically. Many religion books are like picture books because often the accompanying pictures and art tell as much as and even more than the text about what children are invited to learn.

People to Remember

Repeatedly bringing children and young people together with stories of inspiring and great people is an activity that can enhance their vision of the possibilities in the lives of others and themselves. An unusual book for doing this is *Many Saints, Many Ways: Multiple Intelligences Activities for Grades 1 to 6* by Phyllis Vos Wezeman and Anna L. Leichty (Ave Maria Press, 2003). It draws on the latest research surrounding the concept of multiple intelligences (MI) and offers appropriate exercises, activities, and other lesson ideas that fit each of these eight styles: bodily/kinesthetic, interpersonal/relational, intrapersonal/introspective, logical/mathematical, musical/rhythmic, naturalist, verbal/linguistic, and visual/spatial. The book contains a story of a saint for every month of the year. Although the activities are mainly intended for students in grades 1 to 6, they may be easily adapted for use with adolescents, either in large or small group settings. The beauty of this book is that it addresses the reality that children learn in many different ways in the context of learning about a saint.

The third of a series by Michael O'Neill McGrath is *Patrons and Protectors: In Times of Need* (Liturgy Training Publications, 2002). In this interesting book about saints, McGarth shifts his attention from the role of saints as patrons of occupations to their role as protectors in times of need. Each double-page spread contains a full-color picture of the saint, a sketch of the saint's life, and a reflection on praying to them in such situations as breast cancer (St. Agatha), AIDS (St. Camillus de Lellis), racial discrimination (St. Josephine Bakhita), and dealing with troubled children (St. Monica).

William Anderson's *River Boy* (HarperCollins, 2003) is about a mischievous curly headed boy named Samuel Clemens who became one of America's greatest storytellers. Better known as Mark Twain, he wrote such best-loved books as *The Adventures of Tom Sawyer* and *The Adventures of Huckleberry Finn*.

In *Woody Guthrie* (Alfred A. Knopf, 2001) Bonnie Christensen recounts the life of the composer of "This Land Is Your Land," a song that is sung by school children and remembered by adults. Known as the "poet of the people," Woody wrote more than a thousand songs, most of which reflect the struggles and celebrate the spirit of the American people from the years of the Great Depression to today.

Ann Arnold's *The Adventurous Chef: Alexis Soyer* (Farrar, Straus and Giroux, 2002) tells of a twelve-year-old boy who was expelled from school for ringing a church bell that also served as the local fire alarm. This left him in disgrace at home. Alexis's brother, Philippe, a chef in Paris, invited him to come there as his apprentice. Alexis became a hugely successful chef with a social conscience, cooking for the starving populace as well as for the aristocracy. During the Irish potato famine he created a model soup kitchen in Dublin where a variety of flavorful soups were served. Later during the Crimean War, he worked with Florence Nightingale in the hospital and field kitchens of the British Army, where he reformed the cooking methods of the military.

Pioneer Girl: The Story of Laura Ingalls Wilder by William Anderson (HarperCollins, 1998) is a lovingly told story of the "real" Laura Ingalls, a pioneer girl who immortalized her adventures in the Little House novels about the many covered-wagon journeys she and her family made. Laura's pioneer experiences and classic books have made her one of the most popular and enduring literary figures in America today.

Tales of Dreams, Courage, and Desires Nurture Children's Spirits

On August 28, 1963, Martin Luther King, Jr., delivered his "I Have a Dream" speech. Yet, over forty years later his hope "I have a dream that one day this nation will rise up and live out the true meaning of its creed: 'We hold these truths to be self-evident: that all men are created equal'"—has hardly been realized. Certainly gains have been made but racism continues in both subtle and overt ways. During Black History Month (every February) it's imperative that parents and/or religious educators remember King's dream and read with children and young people his "I Have a Dream" speech in its entirety.

Dreams are powerful! We're exquisitely reminded of this in Langston Hughes's poem "Dreams," which is published in Hughes's *The Dream Keeper and Other Poems* (Knopf, 1994). This is a poem that, I believe, every child might memorize because it has the power to give courage if and when life begins to unravel.

Courage is connected to the realization of dreams, and this needs to be continually summoned forth in our young. A delightful and powerful resource for helping to do this is children's literature. To read about courage in others can awaken and strengthen its presence and activity. It can also fascinate and stir the imagination. Here are some books that do this:

The Man Who Walked Between the Towers by Mordecai Gerstein (Roaring Book Press, 2003) is the true story of Philippe

Petit, a young French aerialist. Once he saw the space between the two tallest buildings in New York City—the Twin Towers— he knew he had to stretch a rope between them, a wire on which to walk. Amazingly, he succeeded, and the image of him walking between the towers lives on just as does the memory of the towers themselves.

In *Morning Glory Monday* by Arlene Alda (Tundra Books, 2003), which was inspired by a real event, a small girl lives with her family in a tenement on New York's Lower East Side. Life is difficult and her Mama is homesick for sunny Italy. How the little girl changes life for her Mama and the whole neighborhood is a poignant story of the transforming power of beauty and the strong desire in a child to make her mother happy.

In *Chachaji's Cup* by Uma Krishnaswami (Children's Book Press, 2003), teatime in Neel's family is always a memorable time. His father's old uncle, Chachaji, is in charge. Chachaji always drinks his tea out of a faded, chipped teacup that had been his mother's. She had carried it, as a refugee, from one part of India to another. Many things were left behind but not the teacup. Chachaji told Neel that his mother "knew if this teacup got to India without breaking, she would get to India without breaking."

One night when it is Neel's turn to do the dishes, he becomes distracted, and the cup splinters into a dozen sharp pieces. How Neel restores the precious cup and returns it to his great-uncle is a poignant ending to a story about family, memories, caring, and love.

My Name Is Maria Isabel by Alma Flor Ada (Aladdin Paperbacks, 1995) is the story of Maria Isabel, a girl in a new school, a new class, in which there are two other Marias. The teacher decides to name her Mary Lopez. Maria Isabel doesn't recognize her new name when the teacher speaks to her and this makes her teacher impatient. The situation becomes even more painful for Maria Isabel when she doesn't respond to the teacher's request for volunteers for the winter pageant. She is further troubled when her parents plan to come to the pageant to hear her sing and she hasn't told them that she won't be singing. Fortunately, the teacher asks the class to write essays about "My Greatest Wish." When she reads Maria Isabel's essay, she understands and makes changes in both the name she has given her in class and in the pageant.

INDEX OF AUTHORS
WITH THEIR TITLES